W9-ADX-201
3 5674 03395941

SOUTH CAROLINA

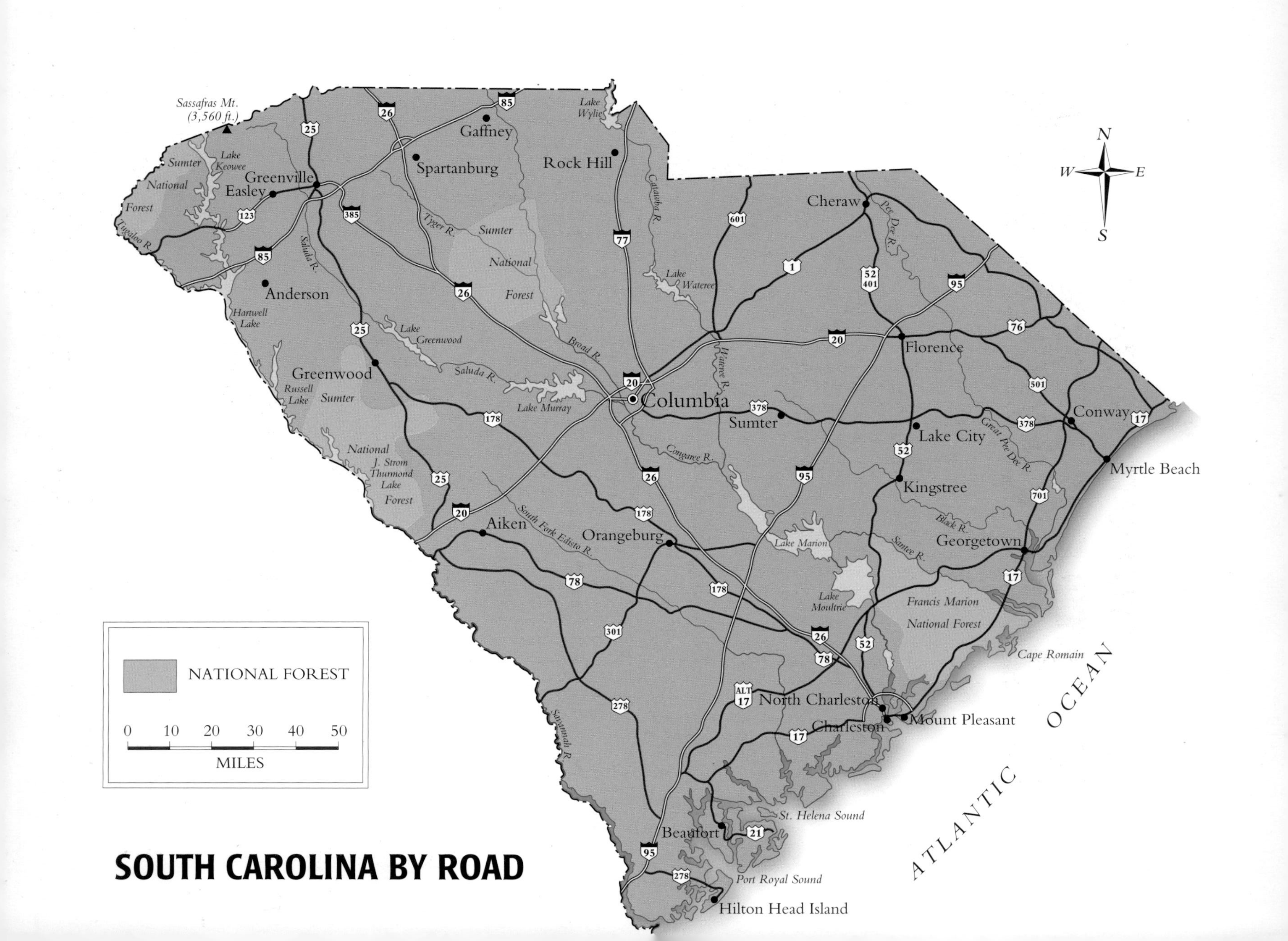
SOUTH CAROLINA BY ROAD
NATIONAL FOREST
0 10 20 30 40 50
MILES
N
S
E
W
ATLANTIC OCEAN
Sassafras Mt. (3,560 ft.)
Sumter National Forest
Lake Keowee
Greenville
Easley
Gaffney
Spartanburg
Rock Hill
Lake Wylie
Catawba R.
Cheraw
Pee Dee R.
Tyger R.
Tugaloo R.
Saluda R.
Anderson
Hartwell Lake
Lake Greenwood
Broad R.
Lake Wateree
Wateree R.
Florence
Greenwood
Russell Lake
Sumter
Lake Murray
Columbia
Sumter
Conway
Myrtle Beach
Lake City
Great Pee Dee R.
Congaree R.
National J. Strom Thurmond Lake Forest
Kingstree
Aiken
South Fork Edisto R.
Orangeburg
Lake Marion
Black R.
Santee R.
Georgetown
Lake Moultrie
Francis Marion National Forest
Cape Romain
North Charleston
Charleston
Mount Pleasant
Savannah R.
St. Helena Sound
Beaufort
Port Royal Sound
Hilton Head Island
25
26
85
123
385
77
601
1
52 401
95
76
20
501
378
17
178
701
78
301
278
ALT 17
21

CELEBRATE THE STATES

SOUTH CAROLINA

Nancy Hoffman

BENCHMARK BOOKS

MARSHALL CAVENDISH
NEW YORK

Benchmark Books
Marshall Cavendish Corporation
99 White Plains Road
Tarrytown, New York 10591-9001

Library of Congress Cataloging-in-Publication Data

Hoffman, Nancy, 1955–
South Carolina / Nancy Hoffman.
p. cm. — (Celebrate the states)
Includes bibliographical references and index.
Summary: Describes the geography, history, government, economy,
people, and culture of this scenic and varied Southern state.
ISBN 0-7614-1065-1
1. South Carolina—Juvenile literature. [1. South Carolina.] I. Title. II. Series.
F269.3 .H64 2001 977.57—dc21 99-058984

Maps and graphics supplied by Oxford Cartographers, Oxford, England

Photo Research by Candlepants Incorporated

Cover Photo: Transparencies / Jim McGuire

The photographs in this book are used by permission and through the courtesy of; *Corbis* : Annie Griffiths Belt, 6-7, 26, 66, 77,84-85; Raymond Gehman, 10-11, 76; David Muench, 13; Karl Weatherly, 18-19; Bob Krist, 22, 82, 100-101, 113; Philip Gould, 58; Tony Azzura, 63; Jules T. Allen, 68-69; Jaquues M. Chernet,87; Michael T. Sedam, 116; Matthew Mendelsohn, 128; Wally McMee, 132 (bottom left); Mark L. Stephenson, 132 (bottom right); Neal Preston, 133; Bettmann, 40 (left & right), 89, 129 (right), 130, 131, 134. *Transparencies* : Robert Clark, 16, 21, 59, 64; Jane Faircloth, 24, 105, 106, 108 117, 119 (bottom); Terry Parke, 62 (top), 125; Kelly Cullpepper, 62 (bottom), 73; Chuck Eaton, 71, 137; Tony Smith, 103; Mike Booher, 119 (top). *Photo Researchers, Inc.* : Jeff Lepore, 17; N. et Perennou, 23; Maslowski, 25; David R. Frazier, 54-55; Jeff Greenberg, 81; Brian Yarvin, 111; Francois Gohier, 121; MH Sharp, 122; Bruce Roberts, 124; John Carter, back cover.*South Carolina State Museum*: 28-29, 48, 94. *Gibbs Art Gallery/Carolina Arts Association*: 32,.35, 44. *Clemson University Libraries, Special Collections*: 34, 42. *Amon Carter Museum,Fort Worth Texas, Marion Crossing the PeDee, William T. Ranney, oil on canvas,1850, 1983.126*: 38. *South Carolina Historical Society*:41. *Library of Congress*: 45,47. *South Caroliniana Library*: 52. *Archive Photos* : Arnold Sachs/CNP,90; Deidre Davidson/SAGA, 96; Bernard Gotfry, 98; Chris Flever, 132 (top); 129 (left). *Avery Research Center*: 92.

Printed in Italy

3 5 6 4 2

CONTENTS

SOUTH CAROLINA IS...

South Carolina is scenic . . .

"It is a very beautiful place. . . . The flowers very fragrant. Orange trees, some kind of Palms, tamarinds, Magnolias, and other tropical plants. Gay birds and butterflies helped to make the pretty scene. Mocking birds abounded." —Union soldier John W. M. Appleton

. . . and it is varied.

"When you have a great variety of habitats, then nature will fill these spaces with a great variety of animals and plants."

—Naturalist Rudy Mancke

Its history is a source of pride . . .

"South Carolinians have always been ready to declare that their land was only a little less desirable than Eden. . . . Like Biblical Eden, South Carolina from early in its history was betrayed by a serpent—the serpent of Pride." —Historian Louis B. Wright

. . . and of shame.

"This was our Ellis Island. Slaves from Africa spent two weeks in quarantine in the Sullivan's Island pesthouse. Then they were brought into the customs house and sold." —Historian Alphonso Brown

South Carolinians are contentious . . .

"South Carolina is too small for a republic and too large for an insane asylum." —James Louis Petigru, South Carolina politician

. . . and they are hospitable.

"Come in, kind friend and browse around our yard; Perhaps by looking Carefully, you'll catch a glimpse of God." —Poet Clarke Willcox

They are passionate about preserving their heritage . . .

"Our historical buildings and beautiful natural areas. These have been left to us to care for, appreciate and cherish."

—Television host Mary Long

"I know I can't save a whole culture, but as an artist I can help create greater awareness." —Gullah artist Jonathan Green

. . . as the future overtakes them.

"I watched the land turn from almost primeval forest to what it is now, which is Manhattan South."

—Author Anne Rivers Siddons about Hilton Head Island

South Carolina is striking country, from its lush mountains to peaceful marshlands to broad beaches. In South Carolina, the old is celebrated and the new is welcomed. Carefully maintained historic landmarks exist next to the most technologically advanced businesses. Sturdy and stubborn, South Carolinians have survived both natural and man-made disasters. Their determination has rebuilt and restored what they continue to love—their home.

1 A SOUTHERN JEWEL

During the American Revolution a fort made of sand and palmetto tree logs helped save the city of Charleston, South Carolina, from a British attack. British cannonballs sank into the fort's soft walls, and the Americans won the battle. In honor of victory, the palmetto tree was placed on the state flag, and South Carolina has been called the Palmetto State ever since.

The Palmetto State looks like a jagged triangle. Its eastern side borders the Atlantic Ocean. Its southwestern side is formed by the Savannah River, which divides South Carolina and Georgia. Its northern side, which borders North Carolina, is the longest.

Covering 31,113 square miles, South Carolina ranks fortieth in size among the fifty states. Despite its small size, it has plenty of geographic variety.

THE UP COUNTRY

South Carolina slopes gradually downward from its western corner to its coast, creating three land regions. The highest two, the Blue Ridge and the Piedmont, make up the area South Carolinians refer to as the Up Country.

In the Blue Ridge region in the northwest, South Carolina's only mountains rise above rolling hills and valleys. The state's highest point, Sassafras Mountain, which is 3,560 feet above sea level, is

In spring, rhododendron and mountain laurel color Up Country ridges.

part of the Blue Ridge Mountains. From its summit four states can be seen: Tennessee, North Carolina, South Carolina, and Georgia.

Not far away is Jocassee Gorges, where sharp peaks tower over rapid waters and a pristine lake. The forests there provide homes to such rare animals as peregrine falcons, big-eared bats, and pickerel frogs. More Swainson warblers live there than anywhere else in the

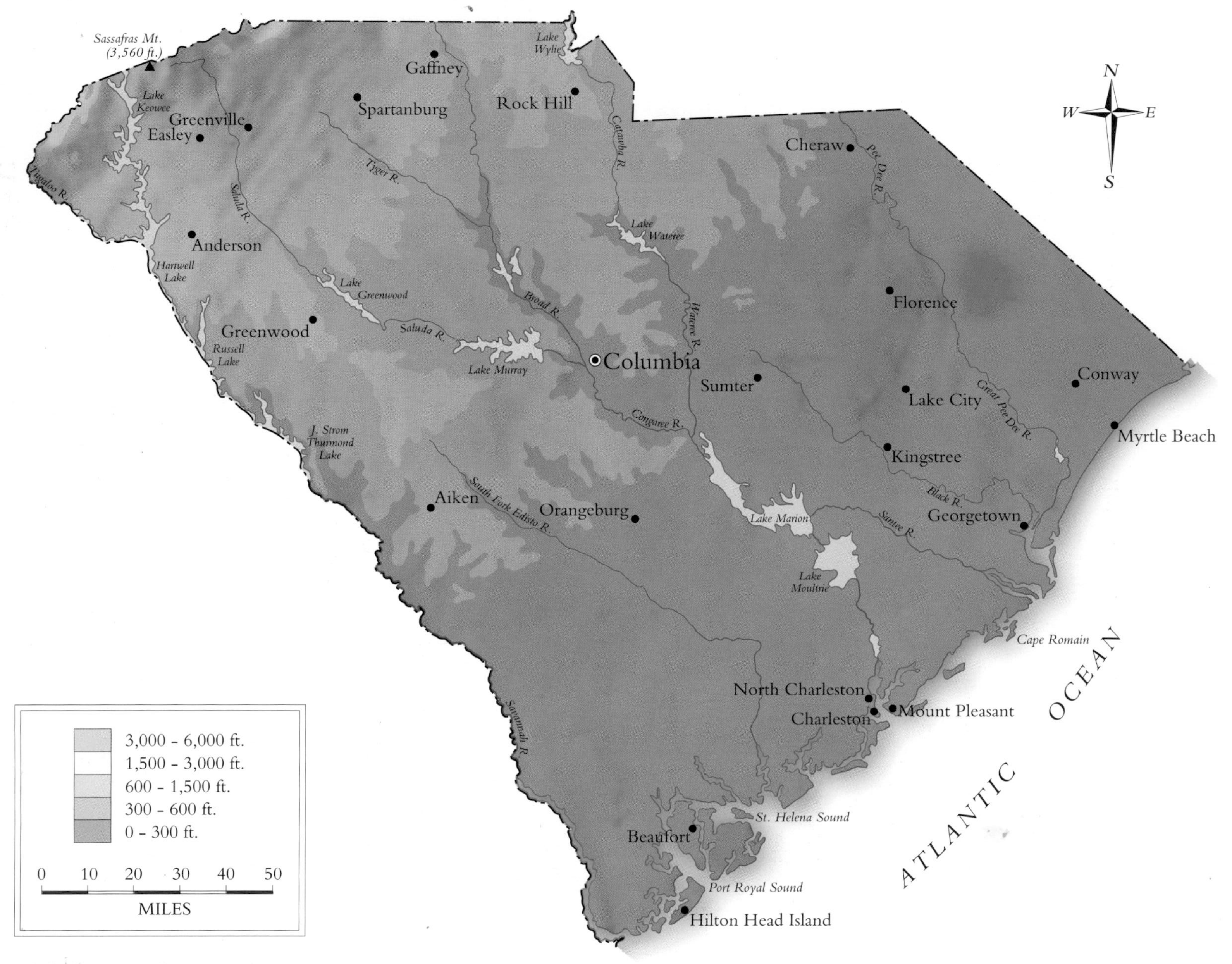

LAND AND WATER

world. The best views at Jocassee come by picking up a paddle for a day of canoeing or shouldering a backpack for a good hike. You can wander the high ridges on a misty autumn day hearing only the sound of your breath and the slow drip, drip, drip of rain from the trees. Or you might stand in the midst of thunder and spray at the base of one of the many magnificent waterfalls that plunge from the highlands on their way to the sea. "This is as wild as it gets as far as South Carolina goes," says Greg Lucas of the South Carolina Department of Natural Resources.

The Piedmont is a wide belt of gentle hills that lie between the Blue Ridge Mountains and the coastal plain. Rivers run swiftly across the Piedmont. Many years ago these surging waters were harnessed to generate power that operated factories. Today, the Piedmont is still home to most of the state's manufacturing. The Piedmont's rivers plunge into rapids and waterfalls when they reach a narrow ledge called the fall line. The fall line marks the beginning of the coastal plain.

THE LOW COUNTRY

The coastal plain is called the Low Country because it is nearly at sea level. Millions of years ago, sharks and whales swam through the sea that covered the eastern half of South Carolina. The coastline was in what is now the middle of the state. Sand hills are all that is left of those ancient beaches. Today, these hills are covered by pines.

Wetlands saturate the middle of the Low Country. Rust-colored cypress trees and ancient oaks cast reflections in the shallow water.

Webs of Spanish moss, a flowering plant with no roots, often hang from the trees. Water hyacinth grows rapidly here, providing shelter and food for all kinds of animals.

As the crow flies, South Carolina's coastline runs 187 miles. But if you count all the bays, peninsulas, and islands, South Carolina has almost 3,000 miles of flat, sandy beachfront property. Over thousands of years, the coast has eroded and rivers have carried silt out to sea. Those remnants of land and small deposits of silt formed

Rich in farmland, South Carolina's Piedmont region is a great place to buy southern delicacies such as peach butter.

South Carolina's swamps are home to many animals, including the osprey.

the Sea Islands, which extend from the Carolinas all the way down to the northern Florida coast. Many children living on the Sea Islands take boats, not buses, to school.

RIVERS AND LAKES

The Santee Cooper region is one of South Carolina's most unusual areas. The Santee is the state's largest river. It is fed by rapid mountain streams and the Wateree and Congaree Rivers. The Cooper, born of seeping marsh and slow creeks, lazily winds through grasses and

Fishing is a year-round activity in and along South Carolina's swamps and man-made lakes.

beneath bearded oak and cypress trees. Dams on these rivers created Lakes Marion and Moultrie. Today, cypress trees still dot these huge lakes and shelter many species of birds. The lakes and rivers of the Santee Cooper region teem with fish, making it one of the finest and most varied fishing and recreation areas in the world.

Other important rivers in South Carolina include the Pee Dee, in the east, and the Savannah, which marks the border between South Carolina and Georgia. Now slowed into a series of lakes with over 110,000 acres of sparkling water, the Savannah is often referred to as South Carolina's freshwater coast.

The Edisto is the world's longest free-flowing "blackwater stream." Such rivers get their dark color from acid released by the tree branches, roots, and leaves decaying in the slow-moving water. The Edisto is popular for canoeing and kayaking.

FROM HOT TO MILD

South Carolinians enjoy sultry summers and short, pleasant winters. In July, temperatures in the nineties are common, except in the Blue Ridge, which is a bit cooler, and along the coast, where sea breezes provide some relief from the heat. "Here we're warm and wet," says Yvonne Michel of Daniel Island. In winter, the mountains protect the state from cold fronts coming down from the North. January temperatures stay in the fifties in the Low Country and the forties in the Up Country.

South Carolina gets a lot of rain—an average of forty-eight inches every year—and sometimes violent storms wreak havoc. One of the worst was Hurricane Hugo, which struck in 1989. Its 135-mile-an-hour winds devastated much of the Low Country, leaving 17 people dead, another 70,000 homeless, and 18,000 miles of road impassable. The storm also uprooted one-third of the state's trees. "After Hugo it looked like a war zone," says Dianne Burn, a Low Country native. "All the trees looked like pencils that had snapped in two."

FORESTS AND FLOWERS

Thick forests cover most of South Carolina. Pines, tulip trees, and magnolias are found throughout the state. Hemlocks, cotton-

Palmetto trees and sea oats dot some of South Carolina's peaceful beaches.

woods, dogwoods, oaks, red maples, and hickories thrive in the mountains and the Piedmont. Oaks, hickories, and cypresses grow in the swamplands, and palmetto trees grow near the coast.

Perhaps the most spectacular time of year in South Carolina is spring, when it seems the whole state bursts into bloom. "Camellias strut their stuff, and, as if that were not enough, Azaleas follow soon to steal the show, to glorify corners where they grow," wrote

Journalist Charles Kuralt wrote of "the psychedelic azalea explosion" every spring in South Carolina.

South Carolina poet Clarke A. Willcox. Goldenrods, jessamines, lilies, violets, and black-eyed Susans also color South Carolina's spring.

The insect-eating Venus's-flytrap grows wild only in the Carolinas.

Its sweet-tasting leaves are traps sprung by trigger hairs at their edges. When an insect flies too close, the leaf snaps shut and digests its prey.

ALL MANNER OF LIFE

Abundant white-tailed deer and foxes share the Up Country forests with black bears, opossums, rabbits, raccoons, and wildcats. Otters play in the rivers and streams, while bass, rockfish, and trout swim in the lakes.

The alluring scent and appearance of the Venus's-flytrap are what make it so deadly.

According to swamp tour guide Sam Kirby, the best time to spot an alligator is in the spring, although the fall's not bad either.

Alligators slink through South Carolina's swamps, which are also home to frogs, water moccasins, and copperhead snakes. This region also serves as a winter retreat for flocks of ducks and geese. Carolina wrens, mockingbirds, catbirds, wild turkeys, and pelicans are only a few of the state's 360 species of birds. The anhinga, commonly known as the snakebird, is plentiful in Low Country swamps. It is called a snakebird because when partly submerged in water, its long neck and beak look and move just like a snake.

Clams, crabs, and shrimp live just off the Carolina coast. So do

FISHEAGLES

When Francis Burn was a child, he used to go fishing with his grandfather. On one of those trips he watched a huge bird pick up a fish and fly away. He heard an old African-American man call the creature a fisheagle—the Gullah word for osprey. Burn never forgot that day. Many years later, he started Fisheagle Tours, which takes people through the Santee Swamp, pointing out wildlife including alligators, anhingas, and of course ospreys.

Adult ospreys are black above and white underneath—the opposite of a bald eagle. They have white heads, except for a black crown and a broad black line from the bill through the eye to the back of the neck. No bird of prey is a better fisher than the osprey. They have unusually long legs, highly curved claws, and feet soled with small spikes to grip slippery prey.

Ospreys sometimes take on human characteristics. Although they usually mate for life, one female with a nest in the Santee Swamp has had several mates. One guide dubbed her Liz Taylor after the actress who has been married eight times. Another new arrival to the swamp is a bit lazy and likes to borrow material from nearby nests to make her own.

Burn keeps track of the osprey population, and apparently it's thriving. When he started Fisheagle Tours in 1994, he spotted only nine nesting ospreys along the Cooper River. Today, he finds thirty.

dolphins and giant turtles. Occasionally huge sperm whales and sharks can be spotted in South Carolina's coastal waters.

SAVING THE LOGGERHEAD

Loggerhead sea turtles have been around for four million years. But unless an effort is made to save their habitat, they won't be around much longer. Loggerheads, which can grow to the size of a large coffee table and weigh four hundred pounds, are found in warm,

Many people offer their time and effort to help save loggerhead hatchlings. One volunteer was amazed that "such tiny creatures become such giants of the sea."

subtropical waters—like those off the coast of South Carolina. After twenty or more years living in the sea, female turtles return to the beach where they were born to lay eggs.

Young turtles are in the greatest danger right after they hatch. Raccoons, crabs, and amberjacks (large fish) all prey on the hatchlings, but perhaps their deadliest enemy is development. At night, away from artificial lights, water appears brighter than land. Scientists believe that this guides loggerhead hatchlings to the water. But streetlights from beach resorts confuse the baby turtles. They crawl toward the lights and often get hit by cars or wander the beach until they are eaten or dry up and die. Keeping beaches dark at night, trapping animals that eat hatchlings, and putting wire screens around nests can help the hatchlings survive. But much work still needs to be done to save this magnificent species.

2 FROM CONFLICT TO COOPERATION

Under the Live Oaks, *by Edwin A. Harleston*

The first South Carolinians were hunters and gatherers. They wandered the countryside more than 11,000 years ago, hunting animals and collecting roots, nuts, and berries to eat. Over time, people in the South Carolina area started farming. They grew sunflowers, corn, squash, and beans. They also began making clay pots. Eventually they built villages.

About nine hundred years ago the Mississippian culture flourished in the area. The Mississippians built great burial mounds out of logs and dirt. Many such mounds can still be seen today.

NATIVE AMERICAN LIFE

By the 1500s, many different Native American tribes lived in South Carolina. The area's mild climate ensured them an abundance of fish and game. The Yamasee, Cusabo, and Coosa lived along the coast. The Edisto, Wateree, Santee, and Congaree settled in the marshes and the Piedmont. The two largest tribes, the Cherokee and the Catawba, were often at odds with each other, usually over land. The Cherokee controlled the mountains but tried to expand their lands into the foothills where the Catawba lived. Both the Cherokee and the Catawba farmed and lived in houses made from logs and tree bark.

EUROPEANS ARRIVE

In 1521, a group of Spaniards set out from Santo Domingo, in the present-day Caribbean nation of the Dominican Republic, to explore the Carolina coast. They dropped anchor in Winyah Bay near what is now Georgetown. A few days later, the Spaniards lured some Native Americans on board their ship and quickly set sail back to Santo Domingo. They presented seventy Indians to Lucas Vásquez de Ayllón, the man who had sponsored their expedition, as slaves. But Ayllón demanded that the Indians be returned home.

Five years later, Ayllón tried to establish a colony in South Carolina. His party probably landed near the mouth of the Waccamaw River, where they established South Carolina's first European settlement, San Miguel de Gualdape. The colonists soon faced a series of problems, including harsh weather and fighting among themselves and with Indians. Many settlers died of disease, including Ayllón himself. Before the year's end, the colony's survivors returned to Santo Domingo.

Early in the 1600s, Great Britain claimed all of North America. In 1629, King Charles I of England gave a region called Carolana (later changed to Carolina), meaning "Land of Charles," to Sir Robert Heath. But Heath did nothing with the region, so King Charles II took the land back and gave it to eight men called the lords proprietors. These men recruited colonists from the British-controlled Caribbean island of Barbados to settle the region.

In 1670, settlers established Charles Town, South Carolina's first permanent European settlement, at Albemarle Point. The Barbadians began experimenting with crops in their new home. They were not

Because of its status as an excellent port, Charles Town became the fourth-largest city in colonial America.

very successful with sugar, tobacco, or cotton. But around 1680, they began growing rice from Madagascar, an island off Africa. Rice thrived along the swampy Carolina coast and soon developed into a profitable export. The people of Charles Town also earned money from trade in furs and deerskins. There was a great demand for such goods in England, where deerskin clothing was popular.

TRADE AND TENSION

The Cherokee and Catawba were the colonists' most important trading partners. At first, the Indians and settlers coexisted peacefully. But gradually more and more settlers moved into Indian territory, sometimes forcing Indians into slavery as they overtook their land.

In 1715, white settlers built a town on land belonging to the Yamasee. The Indians attacked, killing four hundred people and starting a two-year war. Fifteen other tribes fought alongside the Yamasee. Eventually the colonists won the struggle, and the Yamassee fled south to Florida.

Meanwhile, the colonists faced another menace—pirates were threatening ships at the mouth of Charles Town Harbor. Finally, in 1718, dozens of pirates were captured and hanged, and South Carolina's troubles with high seas treachery were over.

Having battled both Indians and pirates with little help from their government, the colonists were angry. They asked King George I to end the lords proprietors' rule. In 1729, George declared the Carolinas to be royal colonies, ruled by him.

The pirate Stede Bonnet was finally caught after running into a sandbar off the South Carolina coast. He was hanged December 10, 1718 in Charles Town.

COLONIAL TIMES

By the mid-1700s, Charles Town was a city of rich merchants, vacationing plantation owners, and black slaves. Its grand homes were the most lavish in all the American colonies. The city's rich cultural life included theater, music, sumptuous food, and lots of parties. After visiting from Massachusetts, Josiah Quincy wrote, "in grandeur, splendor of buildings, decorations, . . . and indeed almost everything, [Charles Town] far surpasses all I ever saw or ever expected to see in America."

Of course the slaves who made this lifestyle possible did not share in its splendor. Although many of the methods and much of the technology for planting and harvesting rice had been intro-

Charlestonians' favorite pastimes included music and drinking, as this painting by Thomas Middleton depicts.

THE STONO REBELLION

It was the language of drums that sparked one of the most serious slave revolts in American history. On September 9, 1739, a slave named Cato, born in Angola, Africa, led an uprising at Stono, South Carolina. By beating drums, Cato managed to gather a group of twenty African-born men and women. Twenty miles west of Charleston at the Stono River, the rebel band broke into a store and seized weapons and ammunition. The plan was to march south to Florida and freedom. As they marched beating drums and calling out "Liberty!" others joined them, and eventually they become an army of nearly one hundred slaves. They fought their way down the road, setting homes and barns on fire as they went.

But after advancing only twelve miles, they stopped to celebrate their victory. The revelry was premature. The delay gave slave owners time to organize. A white militia surrounded Cato and his band, and after ten days of fighting, about forty African slaves and half as many whites were killed. Eventually Cato and the other slaves were captured and executed.

Following the Stono Rebellion, South Carolina passed a law forbidding blacks to make or have drums. Later, North Carolina and Virginia passed similar laws.

duced from West Africa by slaves, they received no profits from their efforts. A few blacks were able to buy their freedom and became farmers or craftsmen, but most remained slaves.

Compared to the lavish ways of the Low Country elite, life in the Up Country was hard. There, German, Swiss, Welsh, and Scotch-Irish immigrants worked small farms in wild territory. They owned no slaves, had few belongings, and lived in crude log cabins. After passing through the region, minister Charles Woodmason described the typical Up Country diet of pork, corn bread, and clabber (curdled milk) as "what in England is given to the hogs and dogs."

Nor was the Up Country adequately represented in colonial government. Over time, this inequality between the poor Up Country farmers and the wealthier and more politically powerful Low Country residents grew into hostility and mistrust.

FIGHT FOR INDEPENDENCE

In 1763, England ended a war with France that had left its treasury depleted. To raise money, England began taxing its colonies. In 1765, the British passed the Stamp Act, which taxed colonists every time they bought newspapers, legal documents, or even playing cards. This tax so angered the people of Charles Town that some of them vandalized the homes of British sympathizers. England repealed the Stamp Act, but replaced it with taxes on other goods.

While the citizens of Charles Town grew irate, many Up Country farmers remained loyal to England. The taxes hardly affected them, and British treaties helped them keep peace with the Cherokee.

In 1775, the Revolutionary War broke out. About 140 battles were fought in South Carolina before the war's end. Many did not even include British troops. American Patriots, or Whigs, fought Americans loyal to Britain, or Tories, so often that it seemed the colonists were at war with themselves.

In May 1780, the British captured Charles Town. But American leaders such as Thomas "the Gamecock" Sumter and Francis "the Swamp Fox" Marion continued to harass the British, making raids

British commanders were frustrated by Francis "the Swamp Fox" Marion's knowledge of South Carolina swamps and his unconventional approach to warfare.

and then disappearing back into the swamps where the British couldn't follow.

Even the previously pro-British Up Country farmers rallied to the Patriots' cause after a group of British soldiers killed surrendering Americans near Lancaster. On October 7, 1780, a band of Blue Ridge Mountain frontiersmen surrounded British major Patrick Ferguson's encampment on Kings Mountain. Ferguson and nearly four hundred of his men were killed. The Battle of Kings Mountain turned the tide for the southern Continental forces.

The war ended in 1783, and South Carolina became part of a new nation. That same year the city of Charles Town became "Charleston" because South Carolinians thought it sounded less British.

THE GROWING SLAVERY SYSTEM

The invention of the cotton gin—a machine that quickly removes seeds from the plant's fiber—in 1793 increased cotton production and profit in South Carolina. Within a few years, cotton became the state's top crop. As the number of cotton plantations grew so did the need for more slaves to work them. By 1850, 400,000 slaves lived in South Carolina—two-thirds of the state's population.

Threats to South Carolina's slavery system came from both inside and outside the state. In 1822, a free black man named Denmark Vesey planned a slave revolt in Charleston. Vesey and thirty-four of his followers were executed when the scheme was exposed. Meanwhile, the abolitionist, or antislavery, movement was growing in the North. But not all slavery critics were Northerners. Some, such as South Carolina's Sarah and Angelina Grimké, came from slave-owning families.

CRISIS AND WAR

South Carolina first threatened to secede from, or leave, the Union years before the Civil War. In the late 1820s, many South Carolinians were grumbling over increased tariffs (taxes) on imports. The new tariffs bolstered Northern industry, but many Southern plantation owners feared that the tariffs would discourage international trade,

THE GRIMKÉ SISTERS

Although they were born into a prominent Charleston family, Sarah and Angelina Grimké grew up to fight passionately against slavery. After moving to Philadelphia in the 1820s, they started publishing articles and giving speeches denouncing the practice. Because of their activities, they were threatened with imprisonment if they ever returned to Charleston. They never saw their birthplace again. In her article "An Appeal to the Christian Women of the South," Angelina Grimké encouraged women to take up the abolitionists' cause:

> I know you do not make the laws, but I also know that you are the wives and mothers, the sisters and daughters of those who do; and if you really suppose you can do nothing to overthrow slavery, you are greatly mistaken. First, you can read on this subject. Second, you can pray over this subject. Third, you can speak on this subject. Fourth, you can act on this subject.
>
> Speak to your relatives, friends, acquaintances, be not afraid to let your sentiments, be known. . . . Try to persuade your husband, father, brothers and sons that slavery is a crime against God and man.

Sarah Grimké

Angelina Grimké

making it more difficult for them to sell their cotton abroad.

Vice President John C. Calhoun, a South Carolinian vehemently opposed to the tariffs, wrote a resolution claiming that a state could declare null and void any act of Congress it considered unconstitutional. President Andrew Jackson, also a South Carolinian, fought Calhoun on this issue. In 1832, South Carolina declared the tariffs unconstitutional and threatened to secede. A compromise was reached just before Jackson sent in federal troops.

Black slaves toiled in the fields while white masters and overseers weighed the profits of their labor.

John C. Calhoun was a vehement defender of slavery and states' rights.

As the years passed, debates flared in Congress over extending slavery into new western territories. Most Southerners were afraid any restrictions might eventually mean an end to the slave system and their way of life. In 1850, most Southern states agreed to a compromise that would limit slavery to only a few new territories. South Carolina was the exception. *The Winyah Observer*, voicing a common opinion of the day, called the Union "an engine of oppression."

The Republican Party was the party of abolitionists. Weeks after

Republican Abraham Lincoln was elected president in 1860, South Carolina seceded from the Union. Within a year, ten more slave-holding states joined South Carolina in forming the Confederate States of America. Lincoln vowed to preserve the Union by whatever means necessary.

In the early morning of April 12, 1861, Confederate general Pierre Gustave Toutant Beauregard gave the order to fire on Fort Sumter at the mouth of Charleston Harbor. As the shells exploded, onlookers cheered from their rooftops. The Confederates won that first skirmish of the Civil War. But the tide soon turned.

In November 1861, Union forces attacked the South Carolina coast, capturing Port Royal and Hilton Head. Charleston suffered battles, blockades, and food shortages, but it didn't surrender. As the war dragged on, the situation grew bleaker for the Palmetto State. General William Tecumseh Sherman and his Union troops left a path of destruction across Georgia and then turned north and marched to Columbia, South Carolina. In February 1865, Sherman's troops set the capital city ablaze. That same month, Union troops regained control of Fort Sumter. On April 9, 1865, the South surrendered. It was the end of Civil War, but not of South Carolina's troubles.

RECONSTRUCTION

At the war's end, South Carolina was devastated, its cities in shambles, its countryside destroyed. Although the slaves had been freed, most had no way to make a living. "The freed slaves were promised forty acres and a mule," says Alphonso Brown, a black historian. "Some got twenty acres and a mule. Some got twenty

As if they were watching a fireworks display, Charlestonians went atop their roofs to cheer on the first artillery fire of the Civil War. It wouldn't be long until the fire was turned back upon them.

"Above the monotonous gloom of the ordinary ruins rise the churches," journalist John T. Trowbridge wrote of Charleston in 1865.

acres and no mule. Some got a mule and no acres. Most got nothing. Life was hard for everybody."

During Reconstruction, the period right after the Civil War, Northerners tried to control the governments of the states that had seceded. In 1867, Southern blacks began registering to vote under the protection of federal troops. The following year, South Carolina was readmitted to the Union. A new state constitution was written and adopted by transplanted Northerners known as carpetbaggers.

In response to their changing society, some white South Carolinians joined the Ku Klux Klan, a secret racist organization. The Klan used terrorist tactics against African Americans and carpetbaggers. In 1871, Klan violence escalated to the point that President Ulysses S. Grant dispatched federal troops to nine Piedmont counties.

Eventually, white South Carolinians regained power and set about reversing the progress African Americans had made since the war. A leader in this movement was Ben Tillman, who was elected governor in 1890 and U.S. senator in 1894. He helped enact laws that made it more difficult for blacks to vote. Tillman supported the growth of the separation of blacks and whites, called segregation. Signs for "whites only" and "coloreds only" were tacked up on drinking fountains, waiting rooms, and lunch counters.

DEBT AND POVERTY

Agriculture changed drastically after the Civil War. In just thirty years the average plantation shrank from 347 acres to only 90 acres. "Although a few of the more prosperous cotton planters attained moderate wealth," writes historian Louis Wright, "most were lucky if they could boast a servant or two and keep their debts paid." The majority of the state's farmers didn't own any land. Instead, they worked land owned by others, paying them a portion of their profits in a system known as sharecropping. The landlord's profit was constant, but the sharecropper's was at the mercy of weather and other uncontrollable forces. Too often, sharecroppers went into debt just trying to survive.

Life was not much better for textile workers. Most were paid near poverty wages. Their children couldn't go to school because they had to work to help the family. Some mill owners tried to establish better conditions for their workers. In 1845, William Gregg had set up a village named Graniteville, which included homes for three hundred cotton mill workers, a school, and a church. Gregg's employees had the benefit of both a job and a community. But few cotton factories lived up to Gregg's example. Like sharecroppers, textile workers were stuck in poverty.

In 1921, the state's agricultural industry took another hit when an insect called the boll weevil destroyed half the cotton crop. About the same time many black South Carolinians left to work in northern factories, leaving whites in the majority for the first time since before the Civil War.

At this time, many South Carolinians lived in dismal housing and couldn't read or write. Diseases such as smallpox, typhoid, and

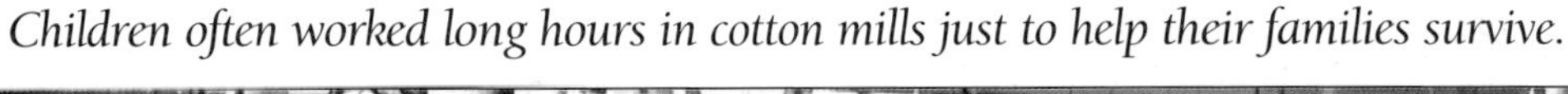

Children often worked long hours in cotton mills just to help their families survive.

WINNSBORO COTTON MILL BLUES

Thousands of textile workers lured down from the Carolina hills to mill towns like Winnsboro by the promise of good wages in the 1920s received a rude awakening. Men often worked seventy-hour weeks with an average take-home pay of eleven dollars. Women made only half that. Attempts to unionize were met with violence and bloodshed. This humorous song was based on the melody of a popular song written in 1919, "The Alcoholic Blues."

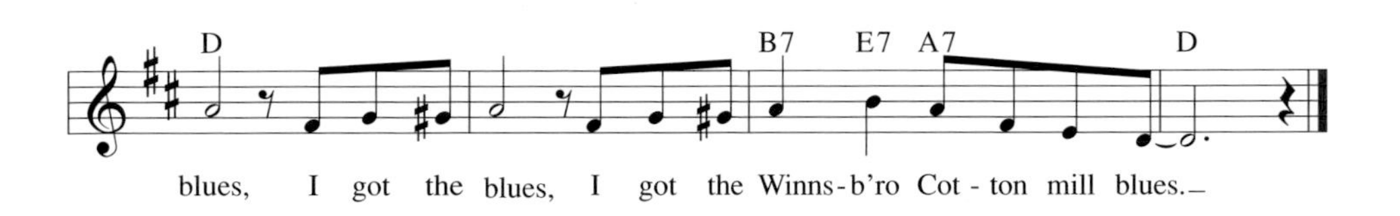

When I die, don't bury me at all,
Just hang me up on the spool room wall.
Place a knotter in my right hand,
So I can keep spoolin' in the promised land. *Chorus*

When I die, don't bury me deep,
Bury me down Six Hundred Street.
Place a bobbin in each hand,
So I can doff* in the promised land. *Chorus*

* strip fibers from a textile machine

malaria ran rampant. South Carolina native Sam Kirby remembers his grandmother telling him that when she was growing up, four out of five schoolchildren had malaria. "My grandmother was the only one of the kids in her family who didn't have it," said Kirby. During the 1920s and 1930s, dams were built on many South Carolina rivers, in part to kill the mosquito population in the surrounding swamps, since the mosquitoes often carried disease.

In the 1930s, South Carolina's struggling economy took an even worse turn. Like the rest of the country, the Palmetto State fell victim to the Great Depression. Factories closed, leaving already

Cotton was still picked by hand in the 1930s, a practice that didn't change until after World War II.

poor textile workers with no means of support. And farmers suffered as the price of cotton hit rock bottom.

It took a long time, but slowly life improved in South Carolina. Vaccinations helped curb disease, funds for schools and medical facilities were found, and new roads and highways were built. President Franklin Roosevelt's New Deal legislation created job programs that put many people back to work and helped cotton farmers reclaim their land. After the United States entered World War II in 1941, several military bases opened in and around Charleston, providing more jobs.

THE LONG ROAD TO INTEGRATION

"South Carolina is now the only state which conducts a primary election solely for whites. It is time for South Carolina to rejoin the Union," wrote J. Waites Waring, a federal judge from Charleston. Waring's brave decision in 1947 allowed blacks to vote in Democratic primary elections from which they had previously been excluded.

Waring suffered because of his rulings. His home was vandalized, and he was shunned by friends and relatives. "We do not live in darkest Africa. We live in darkest South Carolina," he said after anti–civil rights politicians tried to have him thrown off the bench. Eventually Waring and his wife moved to New York.

Waring's decision was the first step toward equal rights for blacks in South Carolina. The process took years, but eventually laws enforcing segregation were thrown out and racial divisions decreased. In the 1960s, South Carolina schools were peacefully

After winning the right to vote in Democratic primary elections, blacks had to take an oath supporting the "social, religious, and educational separation of the races."

integrated, and in 1979 a bronze sculpture honoring Judge Waring was erected in the Charleston City Council chambers.

After struggling with social and economic challenges, South Carolinians have learned to welcome change. "In spite of our faults

. . . South Carolina has astonished itself and others by its progress in our time. We have achieved a reasonable peace among ourselves," says historian Louis Wright. "From the mountains to the coast, [South Carolina] is a pleasant land in which the populace, white and black, can take pride and find satisfaction."

3 WELCOMING CHANGE

The capitol in Columbia

South Carolina's government has grown accustomed to change after resisting it for many years. The state has had seven constitutions. The current one was adopted in 1895.

INSIDE GOVERNMENT

Like the federal system, South Carolina's government has three branches: executive, legislative, and judicial.

Executive. The governor, who heads the executive branch, is elected to a four-year term. The governor appoints important officials and signs bills to make them law. He or she may also veto (reject) proposed laws or parts of proposed laws. The legislature can override the governor's veto by a two-thirds vote. Other elected officials are the lieutenant governor, secretary of state, attorney general, adjutant general, treasurer, comptroller general, superintendent of education, and commissioner of agriculture. All are elected to four-year terms.

Legislative. The legislative branch makes new laws and changes old ones. South Carolina's state legislature is called the general assembly and consists of a 46-member senate and a 124-member house of representatives. Senators are elected for four years, representatives for two.

Judicial. Five justices sit on the supreme court, the state's

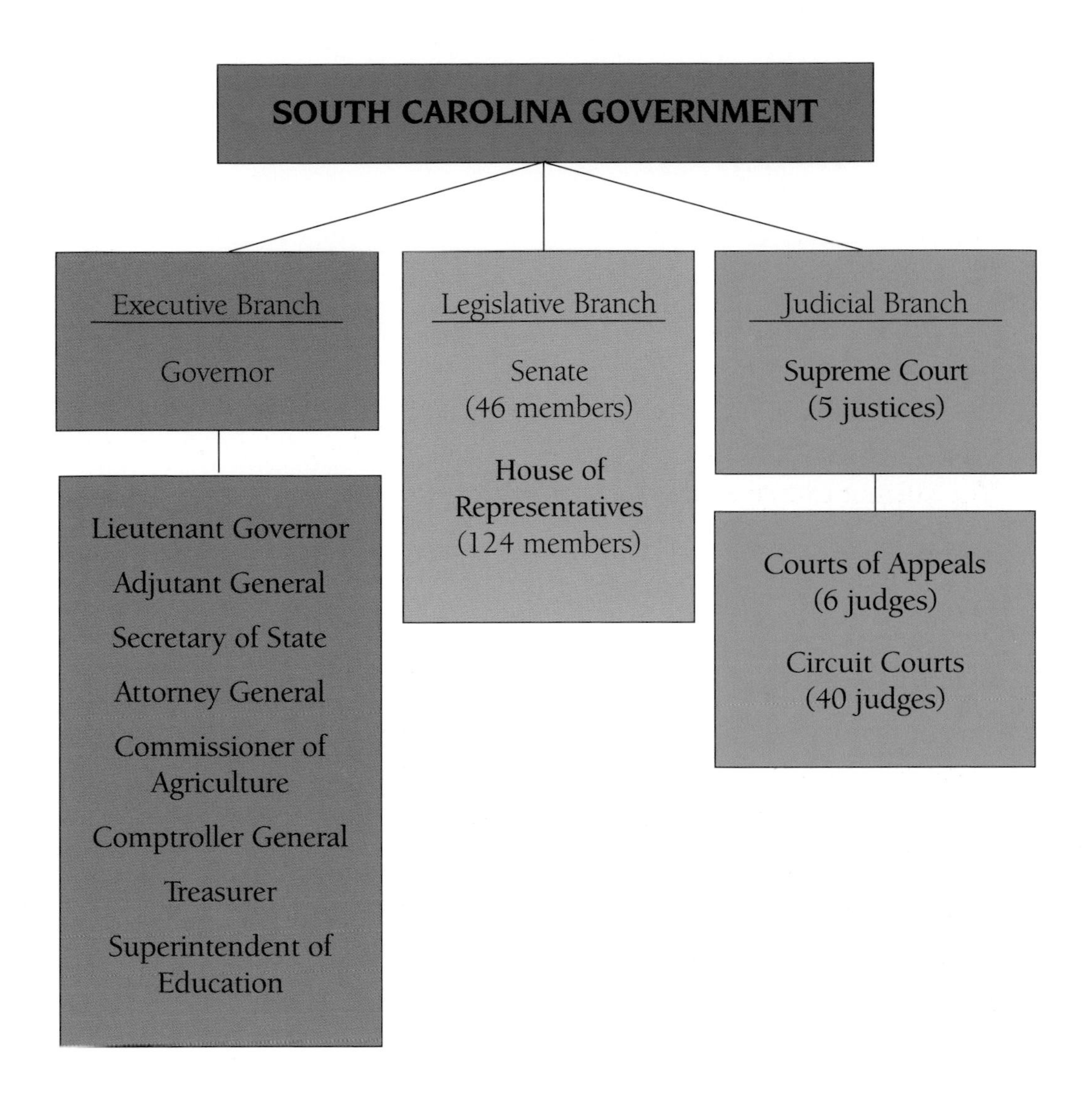

highest court. They are elected for ten-year terms by the general assembly. The supreme court can hear new cases and those that have been appealed from lower courts.

The court of appeals is the state's next highest court. It has six judges and hears cases appealed from lower courts. Most serious cases are tried in circuit courts.

PALMETTO POLITICS

Democrats once dominated South Carolina's politics at all levels. But since the 1950s, the Republican Party has been gaining strength.

Both of South Carolina's U.S. senators are longtime politicians. James (Strom) Thurmond is both the oldest and the longest-serving U.S. senator ever. Born in Edgefield in 1902, Thurmond started his political career as a Democrat but became a Republican in 1964. He was the state's governor from 1947 to 1951. In 1948, Thurmond ran for president as the candidate of the short-lived Dixiecrat Party. Thurmond originally supported racial segregation, but his views have changed as African Americans have become an important voting block in his state.

Lifelong Democrat Ernest (Fritz) Hollings, who was born in

James (Strom) Thurmond has served South Carolina as a U.S. senator since 1954.

THE BOYKIN SPANIEL

Known as "the dog that doesn't rock the boat," the Boykin spaniel is South Carolina's state dog. This rugged little animal can trace its ancestry back to a stray called Dumpy who befriended a Spartanburg banker in the early 1900s. After noticing the dog's natural hunting and retrieving talents, the banker sent Dumpy to his long-time hunting partner, L. W. "Whit" Boykin, who used him for duck and wild turkey hunting in the Wateree River swamp. At the time, swamp hunters' boats were only large enough for one person and a compact retriever. Dumpy fit right in. Frisky and friendly, today's Boykin spaniels look a little like chocolate-colored cocker spaniels. They make wonderful pets as well as excellent hunting dogs.

Charleston in 1922, has been a U.S. senator since 1967. Hollings has worked to improve life for the state's poorest families and has fought for laws protecting wildlife and the environment.

WEALTH FROM THE LAND AND SEA

Although agriculture once dominated South Carolina's economy, it has declined sharply in the twentieth century. By the mid-1990s, only one-third of the state's 24,000 farms had annual sales of more than $10,000. Less than one-half of South Carolina's farmers listed farming as their main occupation. Still, farming is an important second income for many South Carolinians.

Although cotton was once king in South Carolina, today more soybeans, tobacco, and corn are grown in the Palmetto State. Peaches are also a major crop; the only state that raises more peaches than South Carolina is California. Stands selling peaches line the highways of the Up Country a good part of the year. In Gaffney, a water tower shaped like a giant peach can be seen for miles around.

Chickens, eggs, and turkeys are also leading products in South Carolina. Hogs and beef and dairy cattle are raised in the Piedmont and coastal plain.

The two-thirds of the state covered in forests supports a lumber industry. Softwood trees such as loblolly pines are used to make paper and paper products. Hardwoods such as oak, walnut, and maple are cut to make furniture.

Fishing is another active industry in the state. Shrimps, crabs, oysters, and clams are caught off the coast. Inland lakes abound with trout, whiting, catfish, and bass. Fishing is also a growing part

EARNING A LIVING

Agriculture

Chickens

Peaches

Soybeans

Manufacturing

Automobiles

Chemicals

Machinery

Textiles

Tires

Natural Resources

Clams

Granite

Limestone

Shrimp

Gaffney
Rock Hill
Spartanburg
Greenville
Easley
Anderson
Greenwood
Columbia
Cheraw
Florence
Sumter
Lake City
Conway
Myrtle Beach
Kingstree
Georgetown
Aiken
Orangeburg
North Charleston
Charleston
Mount Pleasant
Beaufort
Hilton Head Island

Lake Wylie
Lake Keowee
Tugaloo R.
Saluda R.
Tyger R.
Catawba R.
Lake Wateree
Pee Dee R.
Hartwell Lake
Lake Greenwood
Broad R.
Wateree R.
Russell Lake
Lake Murray
Great Pee Dee R.
Congaree R.
J. Strom Thurmond Lake
Black R.
South Fork Edisto R.
Lake Marion
Santee R.
Lake Moultrie
Cape Romain
Savannah R.
St. Helena Sound
Port Royal Sound

ATLANTIC OCEAN

Today, raising livestock is a bigger part of South Carolina's agricultural economy than growing cotton.

Dairy cattle provide the official state beverage: milk.

Along the coast, shrimp make a good catch for many fishermen.

CELEBRATING THE EARTH'S BOUNTY

South Carolinians like to celebrate the bounty produced in their state. In June, Up Country visitors can sample peach ice cream, hot peach cobbler, peach preserves, and pickled peaches at the Ridge Peach Festival.

The South Carolina Apple Festival in Westminister has been held every September since 1961. Fried apple pies are just some of the treats to taste. Many festivalgoers hang around to see the rodeo, complete with bull riding, team roping, steer wrestling, and bareback bronco riding.

Sweet potato pie is a southern tradition, and some of the best can be savored at Darlington's Sweet Potato Festival each October. In April, the small town of Lamar swells to more than 40,000 for the Egg Scramble Jamboree, showcasing local culinary delights made with or without eggs, along with arts and crafts, a beauty pageant, and a dance. In October, Bishopville hosts the Lee County Cotton Festival. This celebration features a parade, a street dance, a cotton-picking contest, and the crowning of the South Carolina Queen of Cotton.

GROSS STATE PRODUCT: $95 BILLION

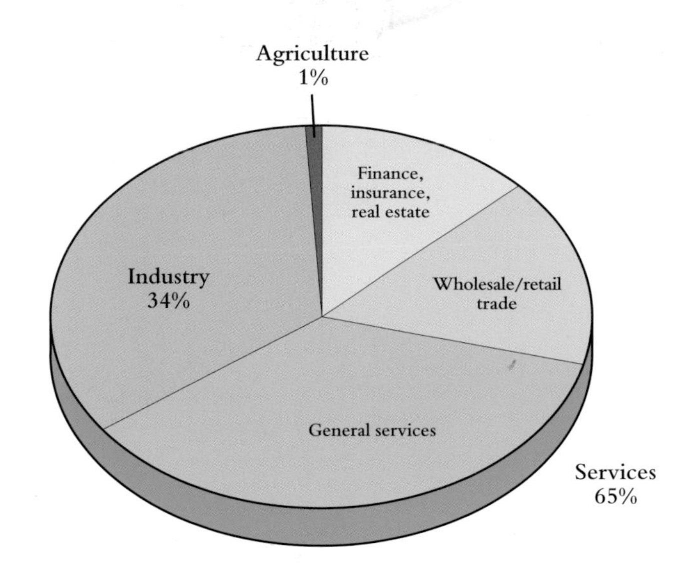

(2000 estimated)

of the state's tourism industry. More than 30 million people visit South Carolina every year. Two-thirds of them head for coastal areas such as Myrtle Beach, Charleston, and Hilton Head. Sea Islands such as Kiawah, Seabrook, and Fripp are also becoming popular.

GROWING INDUSTRIES

South Carolina's economy was based on agriculture well into the twentieth century. When industrialization did come, it brought mostly low-wage manufacturing jobs. Today the average South Carolina factory worker's pay is still among the lowest in the United States.

Manufacturing textiles such as sheets, clothes, and curtains is South Carolina's leading industry. But in the 1980s, many textile workers' jobs were replaced by machines, and more recently some

In a recent survey, South Carolina was one of just a handful of states whose public education systems rated "above average." Here, children learn about good dental health.

South Carolina textile companies have moved their plants to other countries where labor is cheaper.

At the same time, however, many foreign companies have found South Carolina a good place to do business. Almost half of South Carolina's total investments in manufacturing are from foreign countries. Japanese, German, Swiss, and French companies have been building plants in the state since the 1970s. The Up Country cities of Spartanburg and Greenville are a center for international industry. State and local government and business leaders have worked hard to entice foreign companies to South Carolina.

"The mood that has been set over time has created a welcome environment," said James Barrett, head of the Spartanburg County Foundation. "One success seems to follow another." Today, the state's largest manufacturer is Michelin Americas, part of a French company that makes most of the world's tires. In 1992, automobile manufacturer BMW built its first plant outside of Germany in Spartanburg County.

IMPROVING SCHOOLS

"The only way to realize our dreams for South Carolina in the next century is to improve our public schools," said Governor Jim Hodges in 1999. Hodges is not the first South Carolina governor to stress the value of education. In 1984, the state increased school budgets 30 percent. The effort to improve education has paid off. Test scores have risen, and South Carolina was recently ranked second in the nation in school improvement since 1990.

Hodges is working to reduce class size and improve teaching. He has praised educators for adding laptop computers, school-wide networks, and Internet connections to their schools. He has also commended companies such as Policy Management Systems (PMSC) of Blythewood, who "went looking for skilled workers in South Carolina [and] came up short. Instead of continuing to bring in outside workers, PMSC decided to grow its own." The company adopted the Marion Three School District—one of the poorest in the state—pledging to give the district financial support and the kids individual attention. "PMSC plans . . . to make Marion Three the pride of the Pee Dee [region]," said Hodges.

4 SMILING FACES

South Carolinians have a long history of fighting with outsiders and even among themselves. But today they are better known for their friendly and welcoming nature.

GROWING AND CHANGING

Until the early twentieth century, blacks outnumbered whites in South Carolina. But then many African Americans left the state for jobs in the North. Today, about 30 percent of South Carolinians are black and nearly 70 percent are white. But blacks are still a majority in many rural parts of the state. Asians, Hispanics, and Native Americans, many of whom are members of the Catawba or Pee Dee tribes, each make up less than 1 percent of South Carolina's population.

While the majority of people living in the Palmetto State come from a long line of South Carolinians, the number of newcomers is growing. Many people have been drawn there by its economic opportunities and lovely landscape. Katie Mincheff, an engineer and native of Bulgaria, likes the beauty and warmth of the South. She has made her home in Hartsville, where she especially loves being able to garden year-round. "It's a blooming paradise," says Mincheff. Tish and Bob Johnson left a comfortable life in Seattle, Washington, for the Blue Ridge foothills just outside of Greenville. "South Carolina had everything we wanted," says Bob.

CATAWBA POTTERY

Eighty-six-year-old Evelyn George has been making pottery for more than seventy-five years. Evelyn is a member of the Catawba Indian tribe and lives on the Catawba Reservation just outside of Rock Hill, South Carolina. Catawba Indians are the only Native Americans east of the Mississippi still making pottery. It is a skill that has been passed down through the generations.

Evelyn George gives demonstrations of her craft at the Catawba Cultural Center. She never uses a potter's wheel. "I learned how to make pots when I was a little girl from my great-grandmother, my grandmother, and my mother," says Evelyn. "I get the clay from the same place my grandparents and great-grandparents got their clay—down by the Catawba River." Working the clay in her hands, she rolls it, pats it, molds it, and smooths it with water. In about fifteen minutes she has made a seemingly perfect pot ready to be burned in an open fire—the traditional Catawba way. Evelyn makes it look easy; all the while she works she explains the ancient art to a room full of visiting schoolchildren.

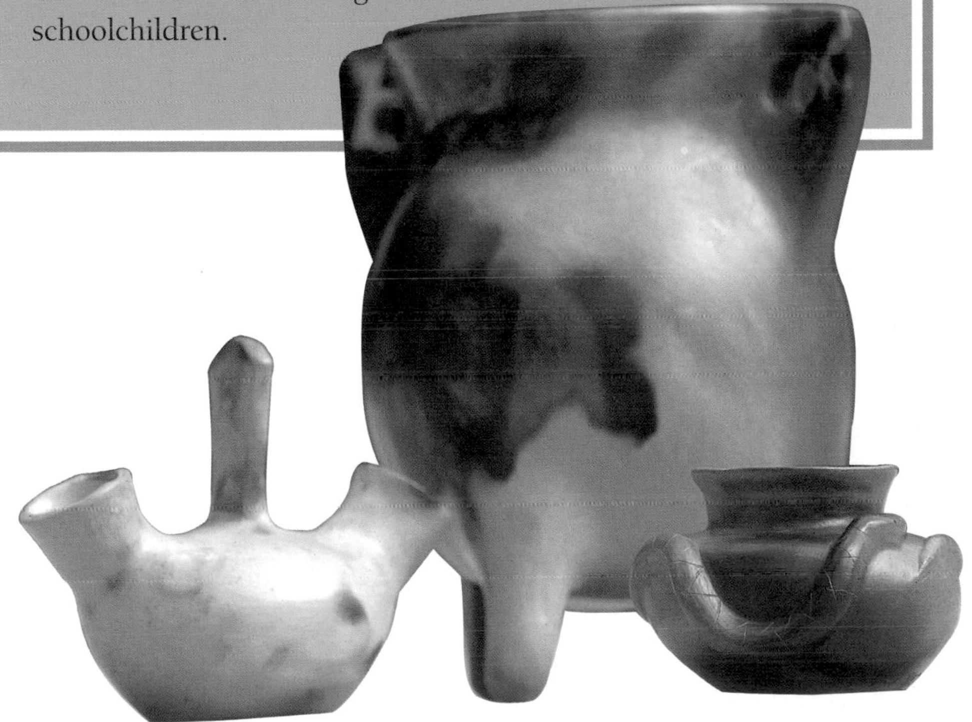

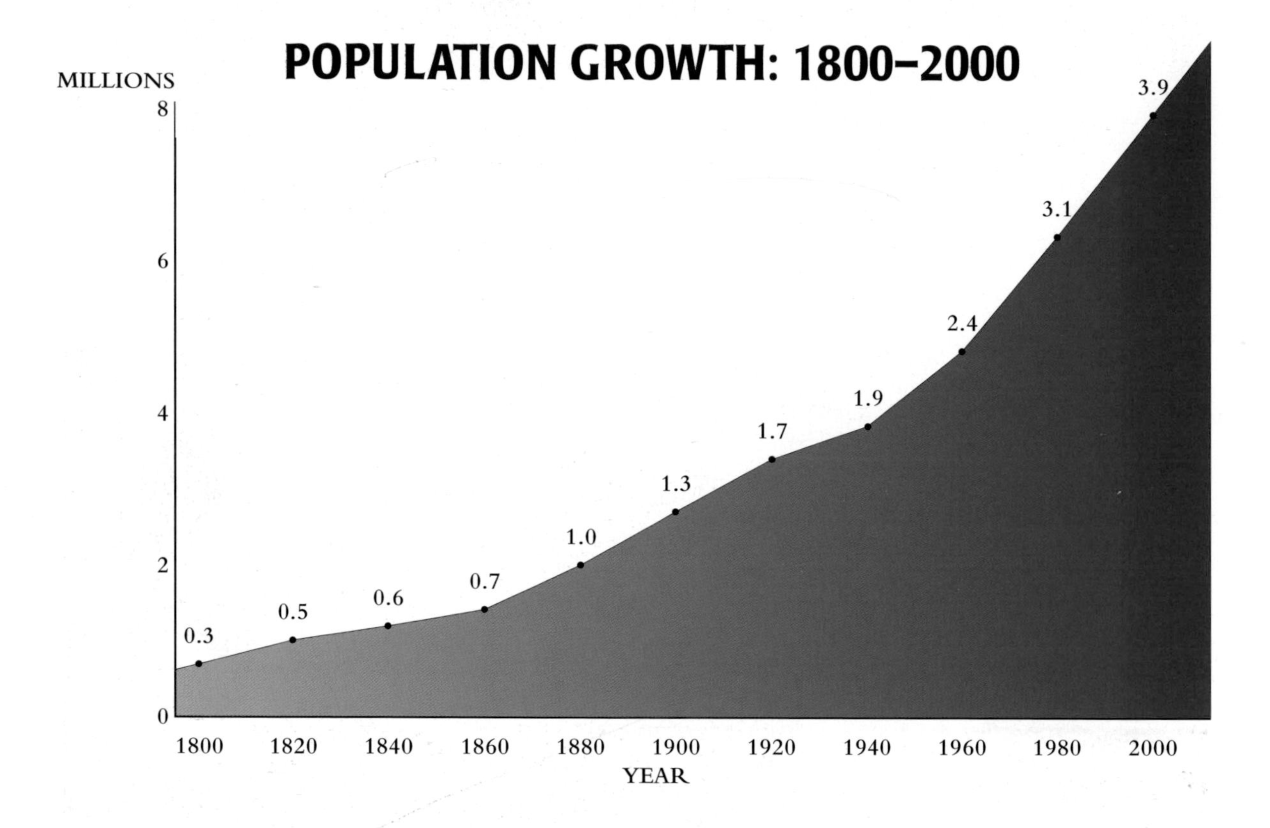

South Carolina remained rural longer than most states. By 1990, however, more than 50 percent of the population lived in cities or suburbs. Today, some longtime residents complain of overcrowding. Sam Kirby puts up with the inconvenience of living in a secluded one-hundred-year-old house outside of Elloree because, he says, "I like being away from all the hustle and bustle." Like its towns, South Carolina's cities are small but growing. Only

"I cannot think of a better place than Columbia for people who have a broad range of interests," said Eleanor Byrne of South Carolina's capital.

NBSC

Columbia, Charleston, North Charleston, and Greenville have populations of more than 50,000.

SOUTHERN HOSPITALITY

"Y'all headed to Blackville?" a local man asks a group of travelers at a gas station along Highway 78. "Well, y'all be sure to drink the water." Blackville's water comes from a natural spring that reportedly can cure whatever "ails ya." In typical South Carolina fashion, the man welcomes visitors and encourages them to see some of the more "off-the-road" sights. Travelers often feel less like tourists and more like neighbors in South Carolina. That's southern hospitality at its best.

When Louise Murdock retired, she moved to Florence, South Carolina, and was pleasantly surprised with her new home: "I never dreamed I could move into a place with such hospitable people."

ROOTS IN AFRICA

"I am a Sea Islander who for many years did not recognize that my religious practices, beliefs, and customs—so many things, in fact, that made up my very being—were African," says Janie Moore, a lifelong resident of Yonges Island and a member of the Gullah community. The word *Gullah* probably comes from the Angolan language of West African. In South Carolina, Gullah is both a language and a way of life that has been preserved by the descendants of slaves brought from West Africa to the islands off the South Carolina and Georgia coasts. Some Gullah are fishers who weave

FROGMORE STEW

Frogmore stew is a traditional Low Country concoction of shrimp, sausage, and vegetables. Have an adult help you with this recipe.

2 pounds Polish sausage, cut into 1-inch sections
1 large onion, quartered
2 quarts water
10 small red potatoes
10 small ears of corn
2 pounds fresh unpeeled shrimp
2 tablespoons Old Bay seasoning
salt and pepper to taste

In large pot, sauté the sausage and onion in a small amount of oil. Add the water and potatoes and bring to a boil. Add the corn, bring to a second boil, and cook for 10 minutes or until the potatoes are tender. Add the shrimp and seasonings and bring to another boil. Cook for 2 minutes or until the shrimp turns pink. Serve with cocktail sauce.

their own nets or farmers who sell fresh produce. Many are skilled craftspeople who make baskets from island grasses or artists who create colorful designs on fabric.

Unfortunately, "progress" is killing this rich culture. Condos, highways, and fast-food chains have displaced Gullah homes. But perhaps the most upsetting threat has come in the form of planned

Sea grass baskets and Spanish moss wreaths are popular Gullah crafts.

communities called plantations. These resorts have expensive homes, stables, country clubs, and golf courses. Their development has raised property taxes by 700 percent since 1990, making it difficult for middle- and low-income islanders to hold onto their land. To the Gullah community, the new plantations can sometimes seem like an echo of the slave plantations of the past. "We have to put up with the 'reincarnation' of the plantation. It is not enough that the resorts are choking us out and forcing us off the island, but they're using a word that symbolizes so much hurt for us," says Yvonne Wilson, who lives on Daufuskie Island.

Despite obstacles, many people born to the Gullah culture are working to pass on their traditions to future generations. "I know I can't save a whole culture," laments painter Jonathan Green. "But as an artist I can help create greater awareness perhaps. All of the change is not bad. But are they throwing out the baby with the bath?"

Gullah is both a culture and a lifestyle. Those who live the lifestyle, such as this fisherman who weaves and repairs his own net, help to preserve the culture.

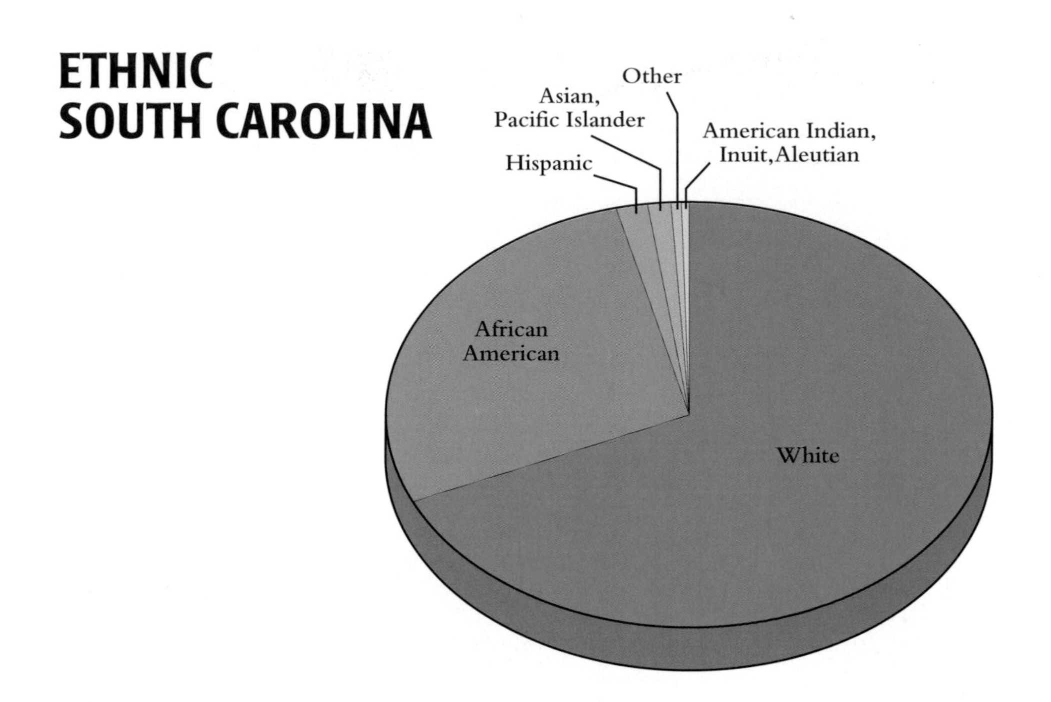

Programs through the Penn Center, which was established to preserve Gullah culture, have helped native Sea Islanders keep their land and their way of life. “The linguists say Gullah is a dying language. Ain’t nothing dyin’ about Gullah,” says Alphonso Brown, a speaker of Gullah. “Just last night, I heard a woman say, ‘Dat food cookin’ smell s’ good mak’ my jaw leak.’”

Each November on St. Helena Island the Gullah culture is celebrated during Heritage Days. The three-day festival opens with the singing of spirituals and a shout, a religious custom in which people clap their hands and dance. Later, participants eat traditional Gullah dishes, while enjoying storytelling, African dancing, basket-making demonstrations, and music ranging from contemporary gospel to old-time slave songs.

BRUH GATOR MEETS TROUBLE: A GULLAH FOLKTALE

In black slave tales, small animals often tricked larger ones. In this story, told with some Gullah words, the rabbit symbolizes the clever slave and the alligator the outwitted master.

Long ago all alligators has smooth white skin like they dressed up in Sunday suits. Bruh Gator float round thinkin' how good life in the river is. With all the fish he can eat he never have to work for a living.

Long come Bruh Rabbit, and Bruh Gator ask, "How you live on land?"

"Don't know, Bruh Gator," Bruh Rabbit say. "We see lot a trouble on land."

"What trouble is?" ask Bruh Gator. "I never meet up no trouble."

"Meet me in the broomsage field after the sun dries the dew up good and I show you trouble," say Bruh Rabbit.

Next morning time Bruh Gator find Bruh Rabbit sitting on top a stump, smokin' his pipe. Bruh Rabbit say, "You stay here, Bruh Gator and I go get trouble!"

He runs to the field's edge and puts his pipe fire to some broomsage. "Lookit that there yonder!" say Bruh Gator. "Ain't trouble pretty!"

Soon the fire hot gets close, smoke gets bad, and Bruh Gator take out for one side of the field. He meet fire. He turn around and meet it again. He shut his eyes, throw his head close ground, and bust through fire to the river.

Bruh Gator get out of water and what he find? His white skin is all burned black and crinkly up. His good Sunday suit gone forever.

"I've learned my lesson," say Bruh Gator. "Don't go looking for trouble, else you might find it."

PRESERVING THE PAST

"I like that old saying, 'Don't know where we are going 'til we know where we've been,'" says Ike Carpenter, a native of Trenton, South Carolina, and a well-known wood-carver. Carpenter makes a habit of keeping family traditions alive. Like his father before him, Ike whittles peach pits into intricate designs, often depicting animals. He also carves spoons. With each handmade utensil comes a story about how it was used in the past.

Preserving the past is an ongoing activity for many South Carolinians. Charleston was the first U.S. city to preserve its historic buildings. And many of South Carolina's smaller communities have followed Charleston's example, gaining much for their efforts. Newberry is experiencing a rebirth two hundred years after it was founded. The revitalization was sparked by the restoration of the town's 120-year-old opera house. "The town was dying and I couldn't let that happen," says James E. Wiseman Jr., a lifelong resident of Newberry who spearheaded the opera house project. After more than a year of work, the opera house opened in 1998 with its first performance since 1952. "The opera house is the catalyst," said Wiseman. "But we aren't just building a building, we are building a town." Newberry now has antique shops, art galleries, a music shop, and some great restaurants. And shop owners are talking about setting their hours around the performances at the opera house.

South Carolinians are passionate about preserving their historic buildings, such as Drayton Hall.

Historic tours of Charleston are considered to be the best of their kind in the nation.

CHARLESTON SOCIETY

Throughout its history, much of South Carolina has been poor; and most South Carolinians unpretentious. Charleston and Charlestonians are sometimes thought of as the exceptions. While displaying the best of manners and southern gentility, some Charlestonians still consider those who are not descended from their pre-Civil War society as outsiders. "I realize there is still such a thing as 'Society' in Boston or Philadelphia," journalist Charles Kuralt once said. "But for sheer disdainful exclusion, Charleston Society wins all the blue ribbons." According to Kuralt, rich newcomers could never be part of Charleston society. "But you are not impolite to the new people?" Kuralt once asked a blueblooded acquaintance. "Certainly not! We wave to them on the street," she answered.

Historic Charleston has some of the most expensive real estate in the world. But few old-time Charlestonians have the means to maintain these mansions. While it is not always apparent, most of the city's historic homes are now owned by wealthy transplanted northerners.

5 THE PRIDE OF THE STATE

Many South Carolinians have made their mark on the nation and the world. Here are just a few of them.

YOUNG ENTREPRENEUR

In the early 1740s, a young woman helped establish a new crop in South Carolina. Eliza Lucas was only nineteen when she began experimenting with raising indigo, a plant that produces a blue dye. After a few years, she harvested a crop and processed it into blocks of high-quality blue dye. At the time, France produced most indigo, and according to historian David Duncan Wallace, "Great Britain detested paying money to the French," its ancient enemy. In 1748, South Carolina exported 134,344 pounds of indigo cakes to England. The crop remained profitable for South Carolina until the American Revolution.

In 1744, Eliza married Charles Pinckney, and they had two famous sons. Charles Cotesworth Pinckney was a Revolutionary War soldier, a member of the Constitutional Convention of 1787, and a leader in the movement to create South Carolina College (now the University of South Carolina). Thomas Pinckney served as U.S. minister to Great Britain and Spain, was a U.S. representative, a general in the War of 1812, and governor of South Carolina.

Known for his eloquent and inspiring speeches, Jesse Jackson has been a strong voice in national politics for decades.

HE IS SOMEBODY

The Reverend Jesse Jackson is one of this country's best-known civil rights leaders. But his accomplishments have ranged far beyond fighting for racial equality. When he ran for president in 1988, political experts said he didn't have a chance. While Jackson wasn't elected president, he proved the experts wrong. He won the Michigan Democratic primary with a majority of votes from both inner-city African Americans and suburban whites.

Jackson has traveled the world helping to win freedom for American political prisoners. In 1999, he negotiated the release of three U.S. soldiers held captive by the Serbian government; in 1990 he helped bring home hundreds of American hostages in Iraq; and in 1984, he won liberty for a U.S. Navy officer shot down over Syria.

For Jackson, the road to national prominence was long and rough. He was born in Greenville in 1941. Growing up in the segregated South was difficult. Jesse had to walk five miles to elementary school when there was a public school for white children just two blocks from his home. He was told not to question the way things were—that could be dangerous for a black child. But his grandmother, Matilda Burns, believed in him. "Nobody's going to think much of you unless you think so yourself. You're as good as the next person and don't you forget it. Promise me you'll be somebody," she told him over and over.

Jesse took her advice. He was a good student and a football star in high school and college. He eventually left South Carolina to attend Chicago Theological Seminary. There he joined the local chapter of the Southern Christian Leadership Conference, a civil rights organization headed by the Reverend Martin Luther King Jr. Later Jackson started Operation Breadbasket, PUSH, and the Rainbow Coalition—organizations that have helped minorities get better jobs, housing, and education, along with a stronger voice in government.

FROM SLAVE TO HERO

Piloting a rebel gunboat past a Confederate stronghold in Charleston Harbor in 1862, Robert Smalls helped seventeen black

When he died in 1915, Robert Smalls was given the largest funeral Beaufort had ever seen. On his grave is inscribed, "My race needs no special defenses. . . . All they need is an equal chance in the battle of life."

slaves escape to freedom. That spring *Harper's Weekly* declared the feat "One of the most heroic, daring and adventurous since the war commenced." Smalls was the first black hero of the Civil War.

After the war, Smalls plunged into politics, representing South Carolina's first Republican Party. In 1874, Sea Islanders elected him to the U.S. Congress. "The men, women and children seem to regard him with a feeling akin to worship," said a Charleston newspaper after his election. Smalls eventually served five terms in Congress.

FIGHTING FOR CHILDREN

Most of her life Marian Wright Edelman has worked to help children and the poor. Born in Bennettsville in 1939, she remembers growing up and being treated as if she and other black children weren't worth much. "But our parents said it wasn't so and our churches and our schoolteachers said it wasn't so," recalls Edelman. "They believed in us and we, therefore, believed in ourselves."

Early on, Marian was taught the importance of service to others. Her father, a Baptist minister, established the first black home for senior citizens in South Carolina. Edelman attended Spelman College in Atlanta, the University of Paris in France, and the University of Geneva in Switzerland. After graduating from Yale Law School,

Marian Wright Edelman has devoted her life to protecting the rights of children.

she became the first black woman lawyer in Mississippi, working with civil rights organizations there and in New York.

In 1973, Edelman organized the Children's Defense Fund. Its goal is "to make sure that no child grows up without food, shelter, health care, a stable home environment and a good education." The organization lobbies for laws that protect and nurture children. "The legacy I want to leave is a child-care system that says that no kid is going to be left alone or left unsafe," says Edelman.

EDUCATORS

Born in 1875, Mary McLeod Bethune grew up in the cotton fields of South Carolina at a time when many people thought educating black children was a waste of time. Mary proved them wrong. During the eighty years of her life she worked tirelessly to help African Americans. "I am my mother's daughter, and the drums of Africa still beat in my heart," she once wrote. "They will not let me rest while there is a single Negro boy or girl without a chance to prove his worth."

Mary eventually graduated from Moody Bible Institute, where she was the only black student, and began her career as a teacher. In 1904, she headed to Daytona Beach, Florida, to establish a school for young black women. She merged her school with another black school in 1923. The result was Bethune-Cookman College, a highly regarded academic institution. In 1936, Bethune was put in charge of a federal agency that helped young black people get educations and jobs. This made her the first black woman to head a U.S. government agency.

Septima Poinsette Clark also devoted her life to education. Clark

Septima P. Clark was actively involved with Martin Luther King's Southern Christian Leadership Conference.

was born in 1898. After graduating from high school, she was made the principal of a school for black children in her hometown of Charleston. While she taught, Clark continued her own education and earned her master's degree. In 1956, the Charleston Board of Education fired her because she tried to help black teachers get better jobs and better pay, and because she refused to withdraw her membership in the National Association for the Advancement of Colored People, a civil rights organization. This did not stop Clark. She began developing schools to teach poor blacks how to read and write. Clark traveled all over the South looking for teachers for her "citizenship schools." During the civil rights movement of the 1960s, her citizenship schools became known as freedom schools.

GULLAH ARTIST

"I first drew on paper bags, which was okay because most of my subjects had brown skin," says Gullah painter Jonathan Green. Green remembers well his 1960s upbringing in the Low Country, watching men weaving fishing nets and women canning or drying food. Most of all he remembers the colors. "The people would wear very colorful clothes, they say to confuse the evil gods—the more colorful the better," says Green. "Color for me is happiness." His art reflects his love of color and of Gullah culture. He paints the people of the Sea Islands going about their lives—braiding children's hair, practicing joyful religious customs, gardening, and traveling by boat.

Green, who graduated from the Art Institute of Chicago, is the first known artist of Gullah heritage to receive formal art training. He has lived and studied all over the world, but he keeps returning to his Gullah roots—in part to preserve the rich culture. "The older people were dying, and I began to see people differently," says Green. "I saw them as a people with a strong link . . . probably the strongest link with Africa of any of the black American people."

THE GATEKEEPER

Part of the charm of downtown Charleston's historic district is the carefully crafted iron gates on its beautifully preserved buildings. "If

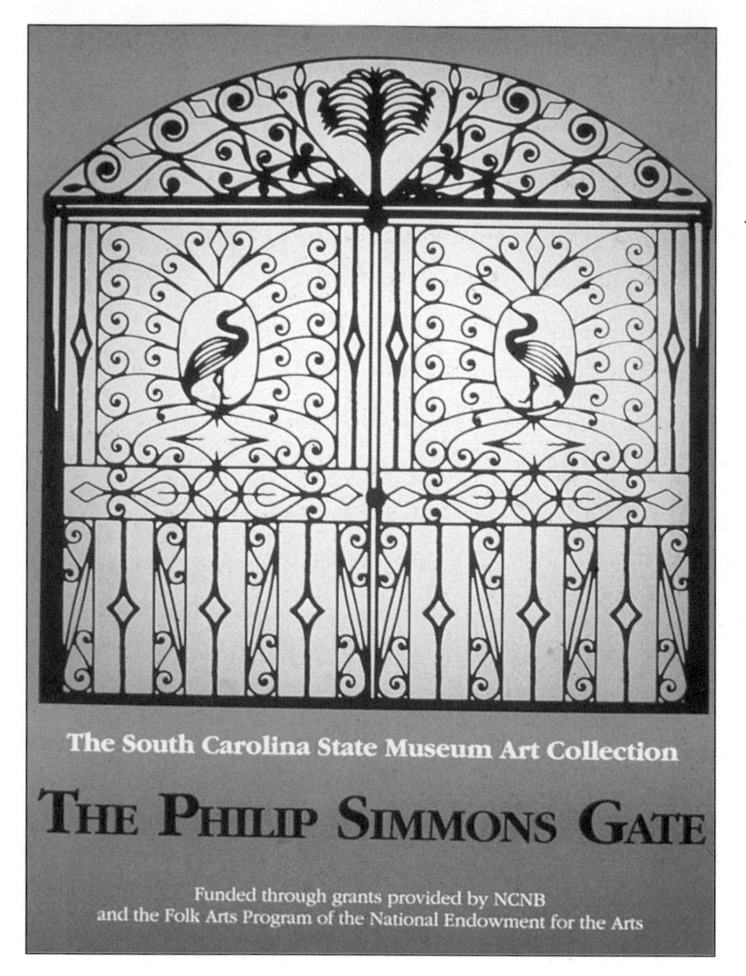

For well over seventy years, Philip Simmons has been firing and hammering out such magnificent iron gates that they are considered works of art.

you see a beautiful iron gate with meticulous curves," says historian Alphonso Brown, "it was made by one of the master blacksmiths of two hundred years ago—or it was made by Philip Simmons." Simmons has been called a national treasure, and indeed his work is on display at the Smithsonian Institution in Washington, D.C. Simmons's work is so famous he is often referred to as the Gatekeeper.

"When I was thirteen," says Simmons, "I used to stand in the door of the blacksmith shop and see the red-hot fire and see the sparks flying and I liked that." The blacksmith let him help out, and before long he began shoeing horses. But times were changing, and cars and trucks were replacing horses. So Simmons started making gates, fences, and window guards. Apart from the Smithsonian, his gates can be seen at the South Carolina State Museum in Columbia, the Charleston Visitor Center, all over Charleston's historic district, and indeed all over the country. "When people leave their Charleston mansions they take their Philip Simmons gates with them," says Brown. Simmons made a valentine gate for his church, St. John's Reformed Episcopal, because he says that is where his heart is.

Born in 1912, Simmons is semiretired now. "The doctor says don't do any heavy work, but I may make some more gates yet," says Simmons. "You know who my competitor is now? Father Time."

GOTTA DANCE

Although Stanley Donen directed twenty-eight films, many people remember him best for the spry song-and-dance routine he performed after accepting an Academy Award in 1998. The award was given to Donen "in appreciation of a body of work marked by grace, elegance, wit and visual innovation."

Stanley Donen was born in Columbia in 1924. When he was nine, he saw *Flying Down to Rio* with Fred Astaire and Ginger Rogers. Captivated by the dancing, he would spend hours at the local theater until his father came to take him home. After finishing high school, he headed for New York City. There he won a role in the chorus of the Broadway musical *Pal Joey*, starring Gene Kelly. Eventually both Kelly and Donen left for Hollywood, where they codirected two classic musicals, *On the Town* and *Singin' in the Rain*.

Stanley Donen codirected what many believe to be the best movie musical ever made: Singin' in the Rain.

Later Donen directed *Royal Wedding*, for which he built a room in a rotating steel cylinder so it would look like Fred Astaire was dancing on the walls and the ceiling. Donen also directed nonmusicals such as *Charade* and *Two for the Road*, both starring Audrey Hepburn.

JAZZ LEGEND

The King of Bebop was born in Cheraw, South Carolina, in 1917. John Birks "Dizzy" Gillespie was a trumpet player and composer

HOLLYWILD

Not all movie stars live and work in Southern California. Many can be found in the small Up Country town of Inman. Some of these "celebrities" are known for playing growling villains, others for being fleet-footed saviors, and one for putting his head in the sand on cue. They are all residents of Hollywild Animal Park. Part zoo and part training facility, Hollywild is owned by David Meeks—"Can Do" Meeks as he is known in the entertainment industry. The collection of more than five hundred animals includes Tank the white rhinoceros, one of two "working" white rhinos in the country; J.R. the black panther, star of many Carolina Panthers events in the National Football League; Ozzie the ostrich; Dominique the Asian water buffalo; Pongo the orangutan; and Chewy the African lion, one of the live models Walt Disney artists used to animate *The Lion King*.

Hollywild has provided talent for countless commercials and more than sixty movies including *The Big Chill*, *Monkey Shines*, and *The Last of the Mohicans*. More and more movie companies are coming to South Carolina to shoot scenes with the animals. "We try to do as much as we can on-site," says Dan Nash, who works at Hollywild. "It saves the producers a lot of money."

who played with jazz greats Cab Calloway and Duke Ellington before forming his own band.

With his puffed cheeks and bent trumpet (it didn't get that way on purpose—someone sat on it), Dizzy Gillespie became an icon in the jazz world. When Gillespie and saxophonist Charlie "Bird" Parker started playing a fast and complicated form of music known as bebop, they were far from a hit. But Gillespie's belief in this new style of music eventually won over listeners and critics alike. The

Dizzy Gillespie played the trumpet like nobody else.

jazz world lost a great trumpeter and musical innovator when Gillespie died in 1993.

BASEBALL GIANTS

"The induction of a native son of Camden into that great Hall was a well-deserved tribute," Governor Jim Hodges said of Larry Doby, who was admitted to the National Baseball Hall of Fame in 1998. When Doby joined the Cleveland Indians in 1947, he became the American League's first black player and major league baseball's second black player after Jackie Robinson. Doby led the American League in homers in 1952 and 1954. In 1978, he became manager of the Chicago White Sox.

Born Joseph Jefferson Wofford Jackson in 1889 in Pickens County, "Shoeless Joe" Jackson grew up to symbolize the best and the worst of baseball. When Joe was six years old, the family moved to Brandon. There, like others his age, Joe was put to work in a textile mill. He eventually escaped the mill's whirring machinery and dust by playing baseball in the Textile League. He could neither read nor write, but his athletic talent impressed everyone. Baseball greats Ty Cobb and Babe Ruth both said Jackson was the "greatest natural hitter" of the game. Eventually Shoeless Joe made it all the way to the Chicago White Sox.

In 1919, the Cincinnati Reds defeated the White Sox in the World Series. The following year, eight Chicago players including Jackson were banned from baseball amid accusations that they "threw" the series in exchange for bribes from professional gamblers. Losing the right to play was the tragedy of Jackson's life: "Baseball gave me my greatest thrill when I was up there hitting, running, fielding and throwing," Jackson once said. "I hardly know which was my biggest single thrill." Jackson maintained his innocence to his dying day, and many agreed that he gave his best in the 1919 series.

6 BEAUTIFUL PLACES

Hike up a mountain, kayak down a rushing river, fish in a swamp, or take a walk on the beach—you can do it all in South Carolina. History is well preserved in easygoing small towns and bustling cities. Celebrated gardens thrive throughout the state. "Smiling faces, beautiful places!" proclaim travel brochures, and they are right. South Carolinians not only love their beautiful state, they love to show if off to visitors.

THE UP COUNTRY

The Blue Ridge Mountains rise from South Carolina's northwestern corner. The rugged beauty of this area is protected in the Andrew Pickens Ranger District of Sumter National Forest. Gradually, the Blue Ridge's peaks descend into foothills with fast-flowing rivers tumbling down the mountains. In all, the Up Country contains more than fifty waterfalls. Issaqueena Falls is among the most visited. Legend has it that an Indian maiden, Issaqueena, pretended to leap to her death to escape hostile pursuers, taking refuge on a ledge beneath the falling water. With water plunging nearly 700 feet, Whitewater Falls is the highest series of falls in the East. Raven Cliff Falls, a 420-foot-high cascade, is one of the most breathtaking sights in South Carolina.

Spectacular waterfalls abound in the mountains of the Up Country.

GROWING CITIES

Some of the country's most rapid commercial growth is taking place near Spartanburg and Greenville in the Up Country. Spartanburg has developed an international flavor by attracting many foreign businesses. Visitors may hear German, French, or Japanese spoken throughout this city. Historic preservation is responsible for one of Spartanburg's finest tourist sites: the Price House, a fully restored 1795 brick building was once an inn for stagecoach travelers.

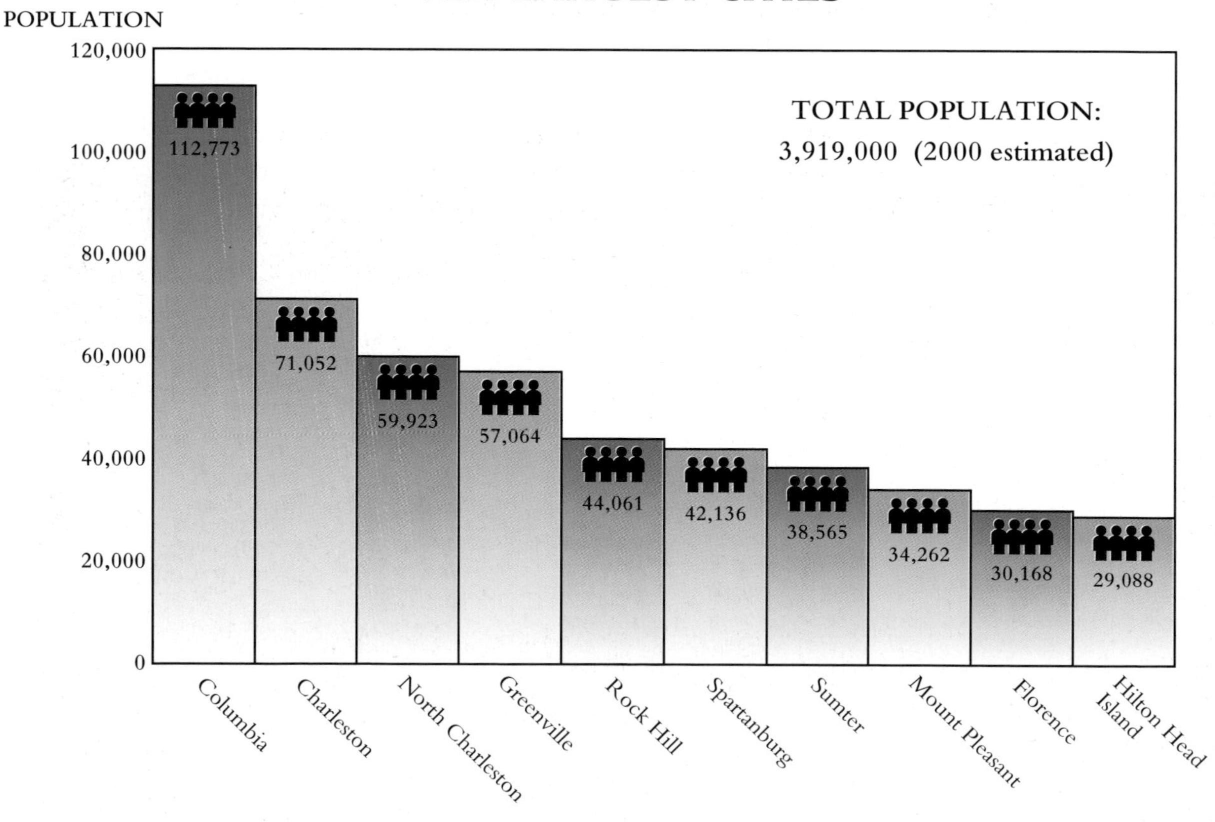

Farther east, the city of Rock Hill hosts the weeklong Come-See-Me Festival every April. At this time, many elegant old homes are opened to the public. Visitors can enjoy some peace and quiet at the city's Glencairn Gardens, discovering acres of carefully tended daffodils, periwinkles, myrtles, and boxwoods, and a lily pond. Or they can cheer on the high-flying competition at the festival's frog-jumping contest.

SMALL TOWNS

Driving through the Piedmont is a bit like going back to an America long gone. Interspersed with woods and grassy hillsides are fruit

Children watch an artist sketch at the Come-See-Me Festival in Rock Hill.

Chester is a perfect example of small-town South Carolina.

stands, boasting the best in South Carolina peaches and apples. Worn gray clapboard shacks—some advertising antiques for sale, others the best barbecue around—dot the roadsides along with firework stands and signs for church retreats. Turn off the main road and before long you are in the middle of a quaint small town.

"Chester County is the sweet distillation of rural South Carolina goodness—front porches, cotton fields, catfish and whippoorwills, dinner-on-the-grounds and friendly downtowns," says television producer Joanna Angle. Chester, the county seat, is charming and well preserved. Chester boasts a pre–Civil War courthouse along with many historic churches and stately nineteenth-century homes.

CENTRAL SOUTH CAROLINA

Aiken is known the world over for its horses. In fact, raising Thoroughbred horses is such a part of life here that there are special stoplights just for horseback riders. The Thoroughbred Racing Hall of Fame occupies the carriage house at Aiken's Hopeland Gardens, which are known for their peaceful reflecting pools and curving paths. Next to riding, golf is probably the area's best-loved pastime. Aiken's Palmetto Golf Course, founded in 1892, is almost as old as golf in America.

Columbia, South Carolina's capital, is the state's largest city and its business, financial, transportation, and education center. Six bronze stars on the statehouse are a reminder that this city endured Sherman's invasion. They are placed on the spots where cannonballs hit the building.

Columbia is home to many outstanding museums. The South Carolina State Museum chronicles the state's human and natural history. The Columbia Museum of Art displays outstanding European art. And the Riverbanks Zoo and Botanical Garden is one of the world's most innovative zoos, specializing in breeding endangered species, such as toucans and Bali mynahs.

Fast cars and festivals are a major part of life in the Pee Dee region, east of Columbia. The Darlington International Raceway is the Track Too Tough to Tame. Twice a year, it hosts overflowing crowds, in March for the Transouth 400 and again on Labor Day

For NASCAR fans, Darlington offers some of the best high-speed action in the country.

weekend for the Southern 500. For more high-speed action, check out the Darlington International Dragway.

Each fall, snowy white cotton bolls cover mile after mile of Lee County farmland. Bishopville is home to the South Carolina Cotton Museum. Exhibits show how the fiber from the cotton boll ends up as the fabric clothes are made from. Visitors also learn about the history of cotton and see old and new cotton-picking machines.

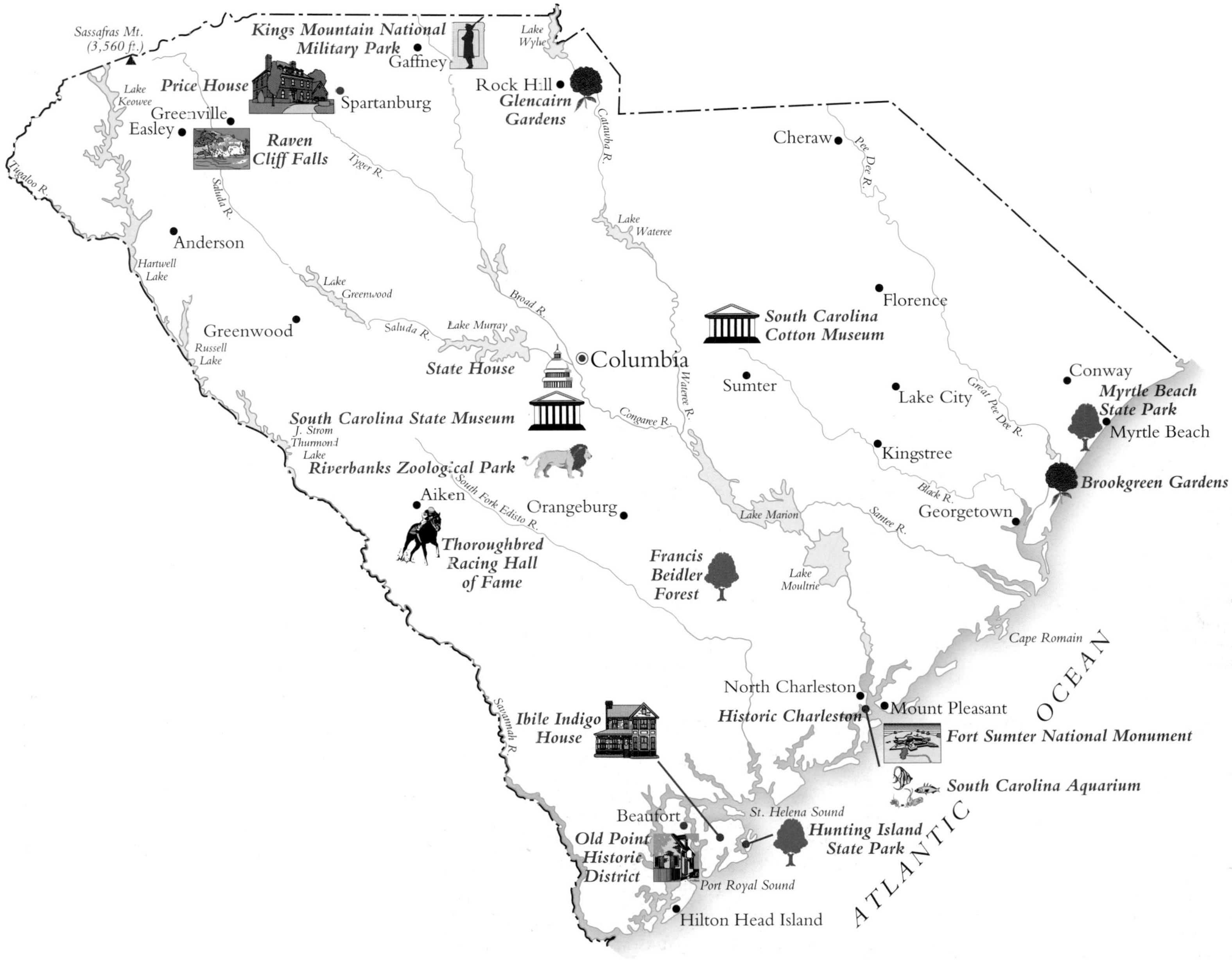

PLACES TO SEE

Sassafras Mt. (3,560 ft.)
Kings Mountain National Military Park
Gaffney
Lake Wylie
Rock Hill
Glencairn Gardens
Price House
Spartanburg
Lake Keowee
Greenville
Easley
Raven Cliff Falls
Tugaloo R.
Tyger R.
Saluda R.
Catawba R.
Cheraw
Pee Dee R.
Lake Wateree
Anderson
Hartwell Lake
Lake Greenwood
Broad R.
Florence
South Carolina Cotton Museum
Greenwood
Russell Lake
Lake Murray
State House
Columbia
Sumter
Conway
Lake City
Great Pee Dee R.
Myrtle Beach State Park
Myrtle Beach
Wateree R.
South Carolina State Museum
Congaree R.
J. Strom Thurmond Lake
Riverbanks Zoological Park
Kingstree
Brookgreen Gardens
Black R.
Aiken
South Fork Edisto R.
Orangeburg
Georgetown
Lake Marion
Santee R.
Thoroughbred Racing Hall of Fame
Francis Beidler Forest
Lake Moultrie
Cape Romain
OCEAN
North Charleston
Historic Charleston
Mount Pleasant
Savannah R.
Ibile Indigo House
Fort Sumter National Monument
South Carolina Aquarium
Beaufort
St. Helena Sound
Old Point Historic District
Hunting Island State Park
ATLANTIC
Port Royal Sound
Hilton Head Island

THE SANTEE COOPER REGION

Swampland is abundant in the Santee Cooper region. The Francis Beidler Forest within Four Holes Swamp is the world's largest ancient cypress-tupelo swamp forest. Nearly two thousand acres of trees tower over clear streams and pools, providing shelter for three hundred species of wildlife. As a wildlife sanctuary, this forest is left totally alone—no attempt is made to lure wildlife to the boardwalk, no animal feeding takes place, no trees or flowers are planted, no fallen trees are removed. It is a swamp as nature intended it.

Lovely gardens bloom throughout Santee Cooper country. Some are planted on purpose, and some by accident. Such was the case with the Swan Lake Iris Gardens in Sumter. Hamilton Carr Bland, a Sumter businessman and avid gardener, wanted to landscape his home with exotic Japanese irises. Despite his best efforts the flowers failed. Bland ordered his gardener to uproot the irises and to dump them around a cypress swamp he had bought to develop as a fishing retreat. The following spring the discarded irises bloomed at the edge of the water.

At Cypress Gardens, what were once profitable rice fields are now peaceful canals reflecting blooming azaleas, dogwoods, daffodils, and wisteria. Visitors can enjoy the lovely surroundings from footpaths or flat-bottom boats. Wildlife abounds in Cypress Gardens. Alligators, otters, and hundreds of kinds of birds can be found there.

Peaceful marshes accentuate the laid-back atmosphere of the Low Country in and around Beaufort.

BEAUFORT AND THE SEA ISLANDS

At night the light of the moon highlights the marshes. Misty morning skies top islands of grass in shallow water. This is the Low Country of Beaufort, Hilton Head, and the Sea Islands. The area's history is everywhere to see and touch—the history of Indians and European settlers, of slaves and planters, of war and Reconstruction and civil rights. Coming into Beaufort it is as if the pace slows down to the clip-clop of horse-drawn carriages giving tours of the Old Point Historic District. The streets of historic Beaufort are narrow. State planners wanted to widen some of them, which would have required deep pruning of ancient oaks' roots. "No thanks!" said Beaufort's citizens; they would rather live with narrow streets.

Indigo was once a major crop on St. Helena. Today, visitors to the Ibile Indigo House, an indigo processing studio, can see demonstrations of traditional indigo dying techniques from West Africa. They include tie-dyeing, using string to tie hundreds of small knots in fabric, and batiking, a method that uses wax to create designs on fabric.

A short drive from Beaufort is Hunting Island, the only barrier island reachable by car that remains essentially wild. A boardwalk through a forest of live oak, palmetto, and loblolly pine leads to a gorgeous beach. A climb to the top of the nineteenth-century lighthouse gives a view of the entire region.

Daufuskie, Edisto, and Fripp Islands all have resorts and unspoiled natural areas. Not connected to the mainland until 1956, Hilton Head Island boomed when a bridge was built. Today, Hilton Head is one of the most popular resort areas in the East. Its

Nighttime tours of Charleston often include some of the city's supposedly haunted houses.

wide white beaches are lined with luxury high-rise hotels and championship golf courses.

CHARLESTON

"Charleston is the spiritual center of the South," wrote one southern attorney. It is also often referred to as the Holy City, because there seems to be a church on every corner. Whatever it is called, this city that survived war and Reconstruction, earthquakes and hurricanes, remains an elegant reminder of the Old South.

At least 850 buildings constructed before the Civil War still stand in Charleston, and most of them have been painstakingly restored. Horse-drawn carriages take visitors through the historic district past homes such as one once owned by David Ramsay, a Revolutionary War hero and surgeon who introduced the smallpox vaccine to Charleston. They might see the house of Confederate brigadier general Pierre Gustave Toutant Beauregard—pirate treasure is rumored to be buried on its grounds. Down by the harbor is the DeSaussure House. From its wide porches, Charlestonians cheered as the first shots of the Civil War burst over Fort Sumter. This and many other homes have enormously thick walls that have saved them from the ravages of time. Most have piazzas—large two- or three-story porches. Before air-conditioning, wealthy Charlestonians slept out on their piazzas in the summertime.

Charleston abounds with culture. In early summer, the Spoleto Festival celebrates the city's fine arts. Operas are performed, new and old plays are produced, the Charleston Symphony Orchestra swells with music, and the Charleston Ballet Theatre puts on three performances a day.

THE GRAND STRAND

From Little River south to Pawleys Island, white sand and ocean surf dominate the landscape. With sixty miles of wide beach, the Grand Strand is a popular summer vacation spot.

History buffs and island lovers should visit Murrells Inlet. There,

THE SOUTH CAROLINA AQUARIUM

Charleston is proud of its newest attraction, the South Carolina Aquarium. This new addition to the city blends into the natural and urban environment while showcasing the state's ecosystems. Projecting two hundred feet out over the Cooper River, the aquarium is a constant reminder of the relationship between the exhibits and the waters of the harbor, where dolphins, otters, and ospreys may be spied. The South Carolina Aquarium boasts many more animals than just those that live in the sea. You can also see Up Country freshwater fish such as catfish, bass, and bluegills, swamp-dwelling reptiles such as alligators and snapping turtles, and residents of the Sea Islands such as loggerhead turtles. Exhibits mimic the varied wetlands of the Palmetto State from a mountain waterfall to a spongy swamp floor to a great ocean tank where hundreds of fish live with sharks and sea turtles.

Christopher Andrews, the aquarium's executive director, hopes it will encourage involvement in the "mystery, magic and spectacle" of South Carolina's environment. "Without a doubt, education is the link between awareness and action," says Andrews. "Our mission is to educate visitors on the many ways in which they can help protect our natural world."

they can tour the Hermitage, an 1842 house that is said to be haunted. According to legend, the ghost of a young woman named Alice returns frequently to a nearby marsh. Alice died after a tragic love affair, and it is said that late at night she searches for her lost engagement ring.

Not far from Murrells Inlet are South Carolina's unique Brookgreen Gardens. Scattered among beautifully tended shrubs and

Myrtle Beach is a popular family vacation spot along the Grand Strand.

flowers are some five hundred sculptures. Included are works by some of America's most famous sculptors, such as Daniel Chester French and Frederic Remington.

Live shows and demonstrations are part of the educational experience at Barefoot Landing's Alligator Adventure. Albino American alligators, dwarf crocodiles, giant snakes, and other exotic wildlife can all be seen at this unusual research institute.

No matter where you go in South Carolina, people will be happy to help you find your way as you share in their state's beauty and rich history.

South Carolina is known for its beautiful gardens. Brookgreen Gardens is no exception.

THE FLAG: The state flag shows a white crescent moon and palmetto—the state tree—against a blue background. It was adopted in 1861.

THE SEAL: A palmetto tree rises above a dead oak tree on South Carolina's seal. The palmetto represents the fort made of palmetto logs that withstood bombardment by British ships made of oak during the Revolutionary War, saving Charleston. The seal was authorized in 1776.

STATE SURVEY

Statehood: May 23, 1788

Origin of Name: Named after King Charles I of England. Carolina is Latin for "Charles."

Nickname: Palmetto State

Capital: Columbia

Motto: While I Breathe, I Hope

Bird: Carolina wren

Flower: Yellow jessamine

Tree: Palmetto

Fish: Striped bass

Animal: White-tailed deer

Gemstone: Amethyst

Stone: Blue granite

Carolina wren

Yellow jessamine

"CAROLINA"

Henry Timrod, who wrote the poem "Carolina," was known as the poet laureate of the Confederacy. The song was adopted as the official state song February 11, 1911.

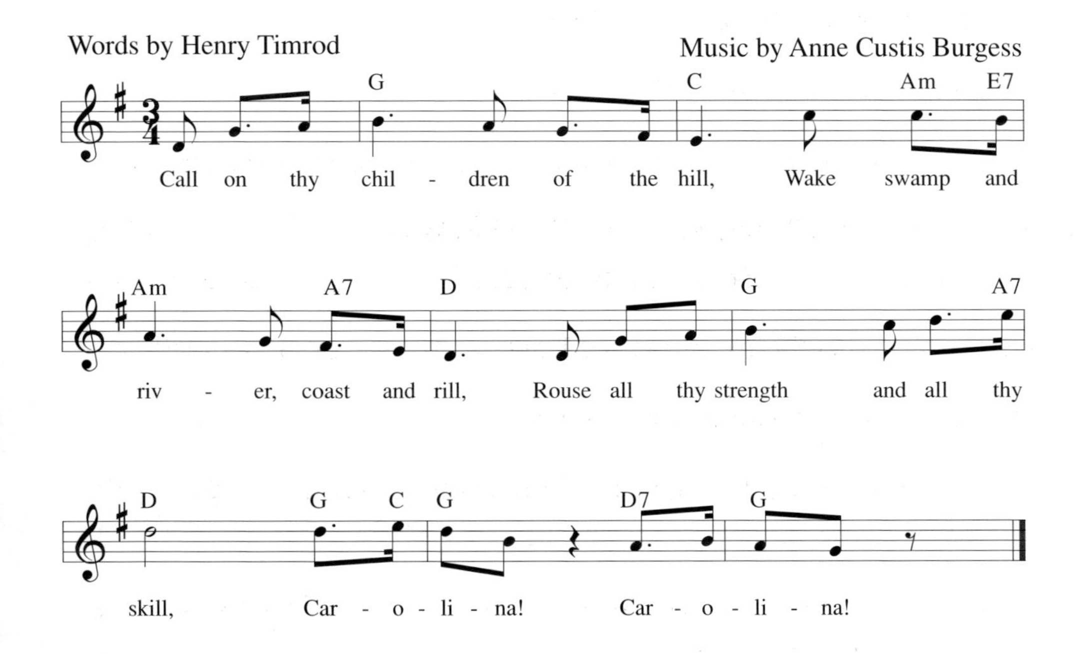

GEOGRAPHY

Highest Point: 3,560 feet above sea level, at Sassafras Mountain

Lowest Point: sea level along the coast

Area: 31,113 square miles

Greatest Distance, North to South: 218 miles

Greatest Distance, East to West: 275 miles

Bordering States: North Carolina to the north, Georgia to the west

Hottest Recorded Temperature: 111°F in Blackville on September 4, 1925, in Calhoun Falls on September 8, 1925, and in Camden on June 28, 1954

Coldest Recorded Temperature: -20°F at Caesars Head on January 18, 1977

Average Annual Precipitation: 48 inches

Major Rivers: Ashley, Broad, Combahee, Cooper, Edisto, Pee Dee, Saluda, Santee, Savannah

Major Lakes: Greenwood, Hartwell, Joacassee, Keowee, Marion, Moultrie, Murray, Thurmond, Wateree, Wylie

Trees: beech, cottonwood, cypress, hemlock, hickory, magnolia, maple, oak, palmetto, pine, sweet gum

Wild Plants: azalea, honeysuckle, mountain laurel, rhododendron, Spanish moss, sweet bay, yucca

Animals: alligator, black bear, cottontail rabbit, dolphin, fox, fox squirrel, raccoon, shark, sperm whale, wildcat

Dolphins

Birds: duck, egret, mourning dove, oriole, oystercatcher, pelican, quail, swallow, thrush, wild turkey, willet

Fish: bass, bream, flounder, grunt, menhaden, rockfish, shad, sturgeon, trout

Endangered Animals: American peregrine falcon, Carolina heelsplitter, Indiana bat, red-cockaded woodpecker, West Indian manatee, wood stork

Wood storks

Endangered Plants: American chaffseed, black-spored quillwort, bunched arrowhead, Canby's dropwort, harperella, Michaux's sumac, mountain sweet pitcher-plant, persistent trillium, pondberry, relict trillium, rough-leaved loosestrife, Schweinitz's sunflower, smooth coneflower

TIMELINE

South Carolina History

1400s The Catawba, Cherokee, Yamasee, and many other Indian tribes live in what is now South Carolina

1521 Spaniard Francisco Gordillo leads an expedition along the Carolina coast

1526 Spaniard Lucas Vásquez de Ayllón establishes San Miguel de Gualdape, the first European settlement in what would become the United States, near present-day Georgetown

1670 English settlers establish South Carolina's first permanent European settlement at Albemarle Point

1698 The American colonies' first government-supported lending library is established in Charleston

1712 North and South Carolina become separate colonies

1717–1718 The pirate known as Blackbeard wreaks havoc on the Carolina coast

1773 The first museum in the American colonies opens in Charleston

1775 The Revolutionary War begins

1780 Colonists defeat the British at the Battle of Kings Mountain, a turning point in the war

1788 South Carolina becomes the eighth state

1790 Columbia becomes South Carolina's capital

1822 Denmark Vesey tries to organize a slave rebellion

1830 The nation's first steam locomotive to be placed in regular service begins operation in Charleston

1832 South Carolina passes the Ordinance of Nullification

1860 South Carolina becomes the first state to secede from the Union

1861 The Civil War begins when Confederate troops fire on Fort Sumter in Charleston Harbor

1868 South Carolina is readmitted to the Union

1893 More than a thousand people die in a hurricane along the South Carolina coast

1895 South Carolina adopts its seventh and present constitution

1921 Boll weevils destroy half of the state's cotton crop

1922 For the first time in more than 100 years, more whites than blacks live in South Carolina

1941–1945 The United States participates in World War II

1948 Governor Strom Thurmond runs for president as the Dixiecrat Party candidate

1963 South Carolina begins integrating its public schools

1974 James B. Edwards is the first Republican elected governor of South Carolina since 1874

1989 Hurricane Hugo devastates South Carolina, causing $5 billion in damage

ECONOMY

Agricultural Products: beef cattle, chickens, corn, cotton, eggs, greenhouse and nursery products, hogs, soybeans, tobacco

Cotton

Manufactured Products: chemicals, electrical equipment, machinery, paper products, textiles, tires

Natural Resources: clams, granite, kaolin, limestone, sand and gravel, shrimp, timber

Business and Trade: banking, real estate, tourism, wholesale and retail trade

CALENDAR OF CELEBRATIONS

Battle of Cowpens Each January, history buffs gather at the battlefield near Gaffney to watch demonstrations of this Revolutionary War battle.

Triple Crown Aiken shows off its horse heritage each March with three weekends of racing.

Festival of Houses and Gardens Visitors can explore Charleston's extraordinary architecture and gardens during March and April, when more than 100 historic homes and gardens are open for touring.

Springfield Frog Jump Young and old alike enter their favorite frogs in this April event to see which can cover the farthest distance in three jumps. The winner goes to the National Jump Off in California.

Springfield Frog Jump

Colleton County Rice Festival Rice-cooking contests and a soap-box derby are part of the fun at this April event in Walterboro, but some people come just to see the world's largest pot of rice.

Spoleto Festival USA In late May and early June, Charleston presents one of the world's premier arts festivals, which features opera, dance, jazz, classical music, theater, visual arts, and much, much more.

Gullah Festival The arts, language, and culture of the Gullah people are honored at this May festival in Beaufort.

Freedom Weekend Aloft Each May, the skies around Anderson are filled with colorful hot-air balloons.

South Carolina Peach Festival Gaffney is so proud of its role as a peach-growing center that its water tower is shaped like a peach. Each July the town celebrates its peachy history with a festival featuring cobblers, pies, and slushes, along with parades, music, and fireworks.

Pageland Watermelon Festival This July festival in Pageland features standard watermelon-related events such as seed-spitting contests. But it is also proud of its more unusual competitions, such as a relay race where the runners must carry 25-pound watermelons, and a lawn-mower riding race in which the contestants must stop to eat watermelon slices.

Okra Strut Each September, tens of thousands of people travel to Irmo to honor that much-maligned vegetable, okra. There are okra-eating and okra-cooking competitions and contests for the longest okra. You might even see people dressed as okra wandering the grounds.

Chitlin Strut Each November, the population of Salley balloons from 500 to 50,000. People come from far and wide to devour several tons of chitlins, the fried small intestines of pigs. They might also enjoy a dance competition and a hog-calling contest.

Candlelight Tour of Homes Some of Camden's most beautiful historic buildings are decked out in holiday finery for the Christmas season.

STATE STARS

Mary McLeod Bethune (1875–1955) was an important leader in improving education for African Americans. In 1904, she founded a school for African-American girls in Florida, which eventually became Bethune-Cookman College. Bethune also served as an advisor on minority affairs to President Franklin Roosevelt. In 1936, she became director of the Division of Negro Affairs of the National Youth Administration, making her the first black woman to run a federal agency. Bethune was born in Mayesville.

John C. Calhoun (1782–1850) was a leading defender of states' rights and slavery. During his long career, he served as a U.S. representative, a U.S. senator, secretary of war, and secretary of state. While serving as vice president from 1825 to 1832, Calhoun argued that a state could declare federal laws null and void. This led to the nullification crisis, when President Andrew Jackson almost sent federal troops into South Carolina after the state nullified a federal tariff law. Calhoun was born in Abbeville.

Alice Childress (1920–1994), a novelist and playwright from Charleston, wrote hard-hitting works about racism and other social ills. Childress began her career as an actor and theater director before turning her attention to writing plays. In 1952, Childress became the first black woman ever to have a play produced in America when *Gold through the Trees* was staged in New York. In 1955, her play *Trouble in Mind*, about racism in the theater, won an Obie Award as the year's best off-Broadway play. Childress also wrote forthright books for kids, such as *A Hero Ain't Nothin' but a Sandwich*, about a 13-year-old drug addict.

Pat Conroy (1945–   ) is a popular writer, famous for his entertaining novels set in South Carolina. Conroy's father was in the military, and his family moved frequently during his childhood before finally settling in Beaufort for his high school years. Conroy attended the Citadel, a military academy in Charleston, and then became a teacher. The year he spent teaching Gullah children on Daufuskie Island became the subject of his novel *The Water Is Wide*. Conroy's other novels, such as *The Great Santini* and *The Prince of Tides*, also include elements from his own life.

Pat Conroy

Lawrence Doby (1923–   ), a native of Camden, became the first black player in baseball's American League when he joined the Cleveland Indians in 1947. A powerful, consistent hitter, he twice led the league in home runs and RBIs. In 1978, Doby became the second black manager in the major leagues when he took over the Chicago White Sox. He was elected to the National Baseball Hall of Fame in 1998.

Marian Wright Edelman (1939–   ) is a leading advocate for children in the United States. Edelman, the first black woman to practice law in Mississippi, worked as a civil rights lawyer in the 1960s. In the early

1970s, she focused her attention on children, founding the Children's Defense Fund (CDF). The CDF does research on anything to do with children and lobbies the government to see that all children get the best child care, health care, and education possible. Edelman was born in Bennettsville.

Joe Frazier (1944–) was once the heavyweight boxing champion of the world. Frazier, who was born in Beaufort, was a relentless puncher, able to wear almost any opponent down. He won a gold medal at the 1964 Olympics and became world heavyweight champion in 1970. His win over boxing legend Muhammad Ali in 1971 is considered one of the greatest bouts in boxing history. Frazier retired from boxing in 1976.

Joe Frazier

Althea Gibson

Althea Gibson (1927–), the first African American to win either the U.S. tennis championship or Wimbledon, was born in Silver. Tall and strong, with a powerful serve-and-volley game, Gibson won both in 1957 and 1958. Gibson was a great all-around athlete. After she retired from tennis, she took up golf and joined the Ladies Professional Golf Association.

Dizzy Gillespie (1917–1993), a native of Cheraw, was one of the greatest jazz trumpeters of all time. Early in his career he played with leading big bands, including those headed by Cab Calloway and Earl Hines. During the 1940s, he and saxophonist Charlie Parker invented bebop, a fast, complex style of jazz. Never before had the trumpet been played with such speed, drama, and surprise. Gillespie was a great showman, famous for his ballooned cheeks. He was also a talented composer, writing such classic songs as "Night in Tunisia" and "Salt Peanuts."

Angelina (1805–1879) and **Sarah Grimké** (1792–1873), the daughters of a prominent Charleston family, were abolitionists and women's rights supporters. After moving to Philadelphia, Pennsylvania, in the 1820s, they became active in the antislavery movement. They gave speeches across the Northeast, becoming among the first women to lecture publicly in the United States. In 1838, Sarah wrote one of the first essays by an American on the subject of women's equality.

Andrew Jackson (1767–1845) was the seventh president of the United States. During the Revolutionary War, 13-year-old Jackson served as a messenger for colonial troops. Jackson became a military hero after defeating the British in the Battle of New Orleans during the War of 1812. Although Jackson was from a privileged background, after being elected president he became known as a leader of the common people rather than the elite. He was born in Waxhaw.

Andrew Jackson

Jesse Jackson (1941–   ), a Baptist minister and civil rights leader, was born in Greenville. While in college, Jackson became an associate of the prominent civil rights leader Martin Luther King Jr. Jackson later founded such organizations as Operation PUSH, which promoted economic development for blacks, and the Rainbow Coalition, which encourages minorities to become involved in politics. Jackson, who twice ran for president, is famous for his rousing speeches.

"Shoeless Joe" Jackson (1888–1951), a native of Brandon Mills, was one of baseball's greatest hitters. Some people say that the great slugger Babe Ruth copied Jackson's swing. Although Jackson had many outstanding years, including helping the Chicago White Sox win the World Series in 1917, he is best remembered for being among the Chicago players who were paid by gamblers to purposely lose the 1919 World Series. Eight players, including Jackson, were banned from baseball for life. Many people prefer to remember Jackson's .356 lifetime batting average, the third-highest in baseball history.

"Shoeless Joe" Jackson

Jasper Johns (1930–), a prominent painter and sculptor, helped originate pop art, a style of art that depicts everyday objects. Johns first became

Jasper Johns

famous for paintings of flags, numbers, and targets. He later often used three-dimensional elements in his paintings. Johns grew up in Allendale.

Lane Kirkland (1922–1999) was the president of the AFL-CIO, the nation's largest labor union, from 1979 to 1995. During his tenure, he worked for equal rights for women and minorities within the union. He also tried to promote cooperation between labor and management. Kirkland was born in Camden.

Andie MacDowell (1958–), an actress born in Gaffney, began her career as a model. When she performed in her first movie, *Greystoke: The Legend*

Lane Kirkland

Andie MacDowell

of Tarzan, Lord of the Apes, in 1984, her southern accent was so strong that another actress had to rerecord her lines. MacDowell had better luck later, turning in impressive performances in such films as *Groundhog Day* and *Four Weddings and a Funeral*.

Francis Marion (1732?–1795), a Revolutionary War hero, was born in Winyah. After the British captured Charleston in 1780, most American troops left South Carolina. Marion stayed. He organized a small group of men who made daring raids on British soldiers and then retreated back into the swamps where the British couldn't find them. From this he earned his nickname, the Swamp Fox. After the war, Marion served in the South Carolina Senate.

Robert Mills (1781–1855), a Charleston native, was one of the country's first professional architects. He greatly influenced the look of Washington, D.C., designing more than 50 buildings there, including the Washington Monument, the U.S. Treasury Building, and the U.S. Post Office.

Jim Rice (1953–), a leading baseball player, was born in Anderson. Rice played for the Boston Red Sox from 1974 to 1989, helping them win two American League pennants. Rice was a strong, quiet player. In his heyday, he was the league's premier power hitter. He led the American League in home runs three times, won the American League Most Valuable Player Award in 1978, and played in eight All-Star Games.

Jim Rice

Robert Smalls (1839–1915), who had been born a slave in Beaufort, became a hero for the Union during the Civil War. Smalls had been forced into the Confederate army. In 1862, he took control of a Confederate ship and sailed it out of Charleston Harbor and into Union hands. He eventually became the highest-ranking black officer in the Union navy. After the war, he served in the U.S. House of Representatives.

Strom Thurmond (1902–   ) has been a U.S. senator since 1954, which makes him the longest-serving senator in history. He is also the oldest person ever to serve in the Senate. Thurmond has a long history of supporting states' rights. In 1948, when he was a Democrat and the governor of South Carolina, the Democratic Party threw its support behind civil rights legislation. In protest, Thurmond ran for president on the Dixiecrat ticket, winning four states. In 1964, Thurmond switched parties, which reinvigorated the Republican Party in South Carolina. Thurmond was born in Edgefield.

Charles Townes (1915–   ), a native of Greenville, won the 1964 Nobel Prize in physics. While working at Bell Laboratories during World War II, Townes had helped develop radar systems. In 1951, he produced the maser, a device that could amplify microwaves. This was an important step in the development of the laser.

Charles Townes

Denmark Vesey (1767?–1822) planned the largest slave revolt in U.S. history. Vesey was born either in Africa or in the Caribbean. In 1783, his owner settled in Charleston. After buying his freedom in 1800, Vesey remained in Charleston, working as a carpenter. He eventually organized 9,000 African Americans, both free and slave, and planned to attack several South Carolina cities. But the plan was uncovered before it began, and Vesey and 34 others were hanged.

TOUR THE STATE

Fort Sumter National Monument (Charleston) You can visit the ruins of the fort where the Civil War began and learn all about its history in a nearby museum.

Patriots Point Naval and Maritime Museum (Charleston) Wander the narrow passageways of the submarine *Clagamore*, marvel at the massive aircraft carrier *Yorktown*, and check out more than 20 other ships and aircraft at this fun and fascinating museum.

Middleton Place (Charleston) This former plantation includes the oldest landscaped garden in the United States, which was laid out in 1741. Besides the glorious flowers, you can see blacksmiths, potters, carpenters, and other artisans demonstrate their crafts and discuss life in earlier centuries.

South Carolina Aquarium (Charleston) Besides lots of fish, you'll also see turtles, alligators, and sharks at this vast aquarium.

Magnolia Gardens (Charleston) Famous for its lavish spring blooms, this garden contains hundreds of varieties of azaleas and camellias. It is also home to miniature horses and thousands of water birds.

Boone Hall (Charleston) Eighty-eight live oak trees line the entrance to this elegant plantation house, which was the inspiration for Tara, the estate in the novel and film *Gone with the Wind*.

Myrtle Beach State Park (Myrtle Beach) Immaculate beaches, nature trails, and great fishing draw visitors to this park.

Brookgreen Gardens (Murrells Inlet) Giant oaks, pleasant gardens, and more than 500 sculptures make this the perfect place to spend the afternoon.

Graniteville Mills (Graniteville) Get a feel for South Carolina's early cotton industry at this mill built in the 1840s. You can also see houses, a church, and a school built for the millworkers.

Penn Center (Frogmore) Originally established as the first school to educate freed slaves in the South, today the Penn Center is a museum devoted to the Sea Islands' Gullah culture.

Hunting Island State Park (Hunting Island) Swimming, surfing, biking, hiking—this park offers endless activities. It even has the only lighthouse in South Carolina open to the public. Climb the 181 steps for a breath-taking view.

Gaffney Water Tower (Gaffney) This town has honored its peach-producing history by painting its gigantic water tank to look like a peach.

Kings Mountain National Military Park (Gaffney) In 1780, American troops defeated a far larger British force at this site, turning the tide of the Revolution in the South. Today, after looking at exhibits and a film about the battle, you can tour the battlefield.

Gaffney Water Tower

Congaree Swamp National Monument (Columbia) You can canoe, hike, camp, and fish in this unusual environment that teems with wildlife.

South Carolina State Museum (Columbia) Feel the fossilized teeth of ancient mastodons, admire a car from 1904, and experiment with laser beams at this wide-ranging museum.

Riverbanks Zoo and Botanical Garden (Columbia) One of the nation's best zoos, Riverbanks is especially proud of its aquarium and reptile exhibits. And don't miss the sea lion feedings.

Francis Beidler Forest (Harleyville) A boardwalk takes visitors through the swamp that contains the world's largest remaining stand of ancient bald cypress and tupelo gum trees. Some are a thousand years old. A canoe trip through the mirrorlike water is even more magical.

Raven Cliff Falls (Greenville) Many people consider this 420-foot-high cascade to be the state's most dazzling waterfall.

FUN FACTS

The Charleston Museum, founded in 1773, was the first museum established in the American colonies.

Wood was so plentiful in South Carolina in the 18th century that only the "hearts of pine"—the centers of logs—were used to build houses. While this method was wasteful, the beams it produced are unusually durable. As a result, many magnificent 200-year-old mansions still stand in Charleston and other historic towns.

In 1825, Charleston native Joel Poinsett, the first U.S. ambassador to Mexico, returned to the United States with a bright red shrub. The plant, which in Mexico had been called the fire leaf or the flame leaf, in the United States is now called the poinsettia. It has become the most popular plant grown and sold in the nation.

FIND OUT MORE

If you want to find out more about South Carolina, check your local library or bookstore for these titles.

GENERAL STATE BOOKS

Stein, R. Conrad. *South Carolina.* New York: Children's Press, 1999.

Thompson, Kathleen. *South Carolina.* Austin, Texas: Raintree Steck-Vaughn, 1996.

SPECIAL INTEREST BOOKS

Branch, Muriel Miller. *The Water Brought Us: The Story of the Gullah-Speaking People.* New York: Cobblehill Books, 1995.

Cooper, Michael. *From Slave to Civil War Hero: The Life and Times of Robert Smalls.* New York: Lodestar Books, 1994.

Ellis, Veronica Freeman, Toyomi Igus, Diane Patrick, and Valerie Wilson Wesley. *Great Women in the Struggle.* Orange, NJ: Just Us Books, 1991.

Jaquith, Priscilla. *Bo Rabbit Smart for True: Tall Tales from the Gullah.* New York: Philomel Books, 1995.

Levinson, Nancy Smiler. *The First Women Who Spoke Out.* Minneapolis: Dillon Press, 1983

McKissack, Patricia C. *Jesse Jackson: A Biography.* New York: Scholastic, 1989.

McKissack, Patricia C., and Fredrick L. McKissack. *Rebels against Slavery: America Slave Revolts.* New York: Scholastic, 1996.

Internet

South Carolina Home Page at www.state.sc.us

South Carolina Educational Television Network Home Page at www.scetv.org

INDEX

Page numbers for charts, graphs and illustrations are in boldface.